TOGETHER
aGaiN

Also by Betty Steele

**THE FEMINIST TAKEOVER:
PATRIARCHY TO MATRIARCHY
IN TWO DECADES**

TOGETHER AGAIN

Reuniting ▫ Men and Women
▫ Love and Sex
▫ Mothers and Children

BETTY STEELE

🔳Simon & Pierre

We would like to express our gratitude to the Canada Council and the Ontario Arts Council for their support.
Marian M. Wilson, Publisher

1 2 3 4 5 • 6 5 4 3 2
ISBN 0-88924-235-6

Canadian Cataloguing in Publication Data

Steele, Betty,
  Together again

Includes bibliographical references.
ISBN 0-88924-235-6

1. Women - Social conditions. 2. Motherhood.
3. Family. I. Title.

HQ1206.S74 1991   305.4   C91-094907-7

Printed in Canada by John Deyell Company

Author Photograph: Peter Caton, Gerald Campbell Studios

Order from
Simon & Pierre Publishing Company Limited /
Les Editions Simon & Pierre Ltée
P.O. Box 280 Adelaide Street Postal Station
Toronto, Ontario, Canada M5C 2J4

To:

My husband,
Gordon Gilmour Steele,
who must be given credit for
the research on which all
my writing is based

My mother,
Mabel Peppiatt Watford,
on whose old-world wisdom
I am often compelled to rely

My children, my family,
my constant source
of all joy and
inspiration

CONTENTS

PREFACE

In 1985, I spent six months attempting to rewrite *Paradise Lost*. I had stockpiled enough evidence to suggest an urgency in diagnosing all the cancerous problems in an ailing society. It was a paradise lost that I believed I had been able to trace directly back to the Women's Liberation Movement. I would seek to prove how the false premises in feminist ideology had led to results as lethal as the fig leaf and the poisoned apple offered Adam and Eve in the Garden of Eden.

I would find that I had neither the audacity nor the skills to rewrite John Milton's classic work; nor could I write a play such as Denys Arcand's internationally acclaimed portrayal of decadence, *The Decline of the American Empire*. Furthermore, I rationalized that it was probably too late to try to entertain, to sugar-coat the truths, and *The Feminist Takeover* was born. It would simply hold a mirror up to society, with a paradise lost, apparently, in every area of our lives: in the alienation of the sexes, with men and women generally, and often officially, in two warring camps; in the "liberated" wildly promiscuous, disease-prone lifestyles successfully disconnecting love and sex; in modern motherhood's abandonment of beloved children, so many of them also denied fathers.

Later, as surely as a great tidal wave recedes, carrying away the detritus, a new world began to emerge on our horizon. A new President of the United States would herald the 1990s as "The Decade of the Family." When, in the first week of his presidency, George Bush was asked, "What has been the greatest achievement of your life?", we heard him answer, "Having all members of our family returning home to us." On *Good Morning America*, March 15, 1990, Barbara Bush declared: "I adore George Bush," and then, "There is nothing in the world like putting your arm around a little child." Here were our new guidelines: love and marriage and children — The Family.

Bringing men and women together again, bringing love and sex together again, bringing mothers and children together again, and restoring the family — the very bulwark of Western society, with all its former moral fiber, its traditional strengths and its blessed security — all this, let us hope, will lead us toward "paradise regained."

INTRODUCTION

We may have entered the most difficult transitional period
in our history, and yet there seems to be a great rejuvena-
tion of the spirit and boundless hope and expectations, as
men and women turn aside from their disillusionment to
seek reconciliation and adjustments in their vision of a
fresh and happier future.

In 1986, I listened to a foreboding speech delivered by
George Gallup of Gallup Polls to the august Empire Club
in Toronto. We were being warned of the very end of our
civilization — as we have known it — if we soon did not
recognize and learn to deal with the problems of our
times, overcoming the "monumental impulses" that were
carrying us relentlessly into the future.[1]

As we entered the 1990s, none of us could deny the far-
reaching influences of the Women's Liberation Movement
on this continent. Foremost Western scholars have called it
a revolution of the most tremendous consequences, echoing Betty Friedan, acknowledged to have introduced the
modern feminist movement with her book *The Feminine*

Mystique, who described this "revolution" as "perhaps the most influential the world has ever experienced."[2]

While Betty Friedan's earliest theories were considered nothing less than revolutionary, she would eventually be seen as a moderate. Radical feminist leaders, wresting the reins from her hands, soon became legally armed and dangerously overpowering. They would be directly responsible in effecting the extreme alterations in an often unwilling society, and many observers believed that a feminist dictatorship was indeed achieved. (This period was chronicled in my earlier book, *The Feminist Takeover*.)

In the 1990s, all tenets of radical feminism are under minute scrutiny and seem to be belatedly challenged. The suffering that the "revolution" has caused has somehow touched almost every human being in our Western world.

Modern philosophers, such as the late Michel Foucault in Paris,[3] are regretting "the denaturalization of men and women" that has taken place during the feminist era. At the same time, my mother, of Huguenot descent, often recalling old French sayings, warns us, "If you kick nature, it will kick right back."

We have all seen it "kick right back" in the continuing desperate problems of a visibly altered and ailing society in which feminist ideology has produced a culture where women are persuaded to become male clones, and men are persuaded to become female clones — with children becoming a secondary consideration. It may certainly be judged as a denaturalizing process, with the most disastrous repercussions for our future generations.

Slowly but certainly men and women have begun to realize that the polarization of the sexes, with men and women eventually divided into two warring camps, must not go on, for it will threaten the very continuance of our species. Furthermore, men and women are again yearning for a traditional type of male-female companionship, and they are more than anxious to put the "single cult" (the words coined by Nicholas Davidson in his book *The Failure of Feminism*[4]) behind them.

The single cult had spawned the "spinster generation," with combative women aloof, and men no longer understanding or trusting women enough for long-term commitments in marriage. (A renowned Yale-Harvard study predicted that women over 30, henceforth, would have little opportunity for marriage.)

The acceptance of the single cult was also obvious in divorce becoming the norm throughout the Western world — divorce initiated by women in 75 to 90 percent of all cases (as reported in major surveys). A large percentage of these women, if they had children, would then face social and economic deprivation often accompanied by unendurable loneliness. Loneliness would become the number one psychiatric disorder throughout North America, with suicide often in its wake.

As statistics recorded a dramatic increase in the divorce rate (500 percent in Canada between 1968 and 1983), the American Association of Suicidology, a research body based in Los Angeles, was noting a 600 percent increase in the suicide rate among the 15- to 30-year-old age group in the United States since 1963. Two-thirds of the 50,000 people who died of tranquilizer overdoses in 1984 were women, although general statistics indicate three times as many men as women commit suicide.[5]

While 50 percent of all marriages in North America are still being dissolved, with the resulting anguish engulfing all members of the families, particularly the children, an urgency to rethink modern attitudes to marriage and divorce in our society has been born.

Allan Gregg, Canada's leading pollster, discussing his book *The Big Picture* on national television (November 19, 1990), spoke of the new conservatism growing throughout North America, with a renewed reverence for long-term matrimony and stable family lifestyles. His polls, which have consistently covered all aspects of a troubled society during the past 12 years, now show a concerted will of Americans and Canadians alike to return to former moral values, including celibacy.[6]

BRINGING LOVE AND SEX TOGETHER AGAIN

It seems that the promiscuous lifestyles, the random hopping from bed to bed, even the so-called "relationships" (which last, on average, only 18 months) are fast going out of style. This is particularly evident in a younger generation's seasoned aversion to their elders' "liberated" morality, which has resulted in their own bewilderment and intense pain. By 1990, half the 18-year-olds on the continent had come from broken homes; many of them would be subjected to repeated pain caused by ensuing broken relationships.

The long-forgotten word "purity" actually surfaced in several instances when a group of 22-year-old university males were asked to make a list of characteristics they were now seeking in the opposite sex. These same young men seemed also determined to find new meaning in the word "love"; it should encompass psychic and spiritual involvement with passion, should be a "love" that could be sanctified in marriage. It would be love and sex . . . together again.[7]

BRINGING MOTHERS AND CHILDREN TOGETHER AGAIN

In 1988, Lowell University in Massachusetts published its astonishing study indicating that one-third of its Master of Business Administration women graduates, formerly in prestigious positions in the business world, had returned to full-time motherhood and homemaking.[8] The results reflected the reality that many women across the continent had already begun to question the feminist ideology that had denigrated the motherhood-homemaking role.

Betty Friedan and all the other so-called feminist authorities — Kate Millett, Simone de Beauvoir, Shulamith Firestone and Carolyn G. Heilbrun, among others — had diligently convinced generations of women that this role was that of a moron. A woman choosing the motherhood-homemaking role was brainless, nothing but a mindless slave of her husband and children: "houseslugs," we were called. These "authorities" had insisted that the only important role for a woman was outside the home, seeking her own individual "identity" and self-fulfillment in singular goals. This was her true right and her "liberation" in the Women's Liberation Movement, her freedom from all the responsibilities of motherhood and homemaking that a former culture had revered as a woman's crowning achievements. Motherhood, of course, would then become the absolute responsibility of the state, as in the Universal Day Care program still promoted today.

While a substantial number of thoroughly indoctrinated women would never lose the feminist mindset, many of them seeming to juggle careers and children with the greatest of ease, others would admit they were simply incapable of the superwoman role expected of them — nor could they deny the "natural" instincts and yearnings of a mother to care for her own young.

Many of these women would slink home apologetically, but they would soon regain confidence in their own decisions and eventually demand such a choice for any woman. Furthermore, mothers at home, they soon discovered, may need far more intelligence and far greater skills than women require in many of their one-dimensional jobs outside the home.

Finding self-fulfillment — and defining a new "identity" — in meeting the myriad psychological, emotional and physical challenges in their new lives, these women began to understand why that wife-mother-family nurturer role had traditionally placed their mothers and grandmothers on a pedestal. Those mothers and grandmothers were revered not only as a source of all comfort and joy within their own families; they were cherished as well for ensuring the future of the world by raising mentally and physically healthy children in a stable environment.

Looking back, many women began to realize that the promotion or the raise they once coveted paled in comparison with the shining faces around a dinner table; here, family communication could be as nourishing as the food on the plates. When they recognized the welfare of their famillies as their instinctive priority, these women found a self-fulfillment that exists nowhere else in female experience. (Feminist theory with its emphasis on the "me-first" goals, or double-priority lifestyles, denies women such self-fulfillment.)

Of course, the problem facing innumerable middle-class women was the compulsive consumerism which had pervaded North America. It had encouraged them to take on commitments, such as large mortgages, which could be maintained only with that second salary. Their expectations, sometimes grandiose and undoubtedly contributing to the evils in that consumerism, would then trap them in lifestyles in which they became extremely disillusioned. The solution for many of these middle-class women emerged in the late 1980s, when statistics recorded a significant number of them retreating to part-time employment outside the home. This retreat, many suggest, will provide a transition to a later full-time motherhood-homemaking role.

The plight of single mothers remains of the greatest concern throughout the Western world. So many of these mothers have simply been victimized by feminist ideology into believing that divorce is indeed a "norm"; that a near-socialist state will provide welfare if support payments are not adequate; that they have the capabilities to "go it alone." (In vain, marriage counselors, courts and well-meaning lawyers have tried to stem the divorce rate, questioning that very word "incompatibility" — which can now cover a multitude of minor grievances.) Yet, afterward, social workers hear one story repeated over and over: "George and I simply got into this terrible habit of battling, day in and day out. No, he never hit me. I only wish now that I had shut up and tried harder and realized that there were worse guys in the world." Single mothers are always searching for greener pastures: for male companionship, as well as for fathers for their children.

Thousands of studies document the adverse effects of divorce on innocent children who can suffer lasting emotional trauma that may damage all adult relationships. The majority of studies reveal that the loss of a father in the life of a child is considered the greatest deprivation. Mothers gain custody of the children in 85 percent of all cases, and in more than 50 percent of these the fathers lose all meaningful relationships with their children. Fathers are routinely, unjustifiably, denied access. The extent of this deprivation became clear in the 1990 census, showing more than 25 percent of all children in the United States living in fatherless homes.

The American Journal of Sociology in 1987 published an article in which Robert J. Sampson and W. Byron Groves analyzed data from a study involving hundreds of British communities. This analysis established "a direct link between single parenthood and virtually every major type of crime." *Psychology Today* featured a survey conducted by Wray Herbert, who had found that "90 percent of repeat adolescent firestarters live in a mother-only constellation."[9] Still other studies show that a majority of members of terrorist teenage gangs come from female-headed households. New York Senator Daniel P. Moynihan in a January 1987 issue of *Time* wrote:

A community that allows a large number of young men to grow up in broken families, dominated by women, never acquiring any stable relationship to male authority, never acquiring any set of rational expectations about the future — that community asks for and gets chaos. This is what we got — chaos.[10]

As it is estimated that more than 70 percent of the elementary schoolteachers and more than 65 percent of the secondary schoolteachers in North America are women, perhaps a continent-wide campaign should be undertaken to attract more men into this field, particularly at the elementary school level. This would fill a specific need by introducing a positive male presence into the lives of fatherless children.

Of course there are all those fatherless children with remarkable resiliency and inherent gifts who become the most responsible of citizens, while children from more traditional backgrounds are often, unpredictably, drawn into a teenage maelstrom of drugs, alcohol or sex, with disastrous results. The incidence of suicide has increased steadily among all teenagers, but there are also children between the ages of five and 12 who have been taking their own lives. A root cause, psychiatrists suggest, is minimal parental attention.

The majority of the thousands of calls that have poured into a kids' hotline established in Canada in 1989 have been from lonely children of all ages, simply yearning for "someone to talk to."

Is there any tragedy in the affairs of humankind that could prove as devastating and as far-reaching into the very future of a whole society as the loss of parents in the lives of their children? Would anyone deny that mothers and fathers and children belong together again?

We know that men and women were put on this earth together, and that they were given specific roles in their gifts of procreation. Historically, there has always been overwhelming evidence that men and women were also given the instincts and capabilities to fulfill those specific roles — as procreators in the continuance of our species, and as parents responsible for the well-being of their offspring.

Yet by 1990 there were many anthropologists and demographers who were seeing a worldwide lack of concern over the probable extinction of certain animal species, matched by a similar lack of concern about an altered civilization that threatened the human population throughout our Western world.

Writers such as Kay Ebeling were laying the blame squarely on the Women's Liberation Movement. In an article entitled "The Failure of Feminism" that appeared in *Newsweek* (November 19, 1990), she explained: "The main message of feminism was: woman, you don't need a man . . . It was a philosophy that made divorce and cohabitation casual and routine."[11]

When feminism offered men and women sexual liberation from all moral constraints, the era of free copulation — sex as a mundane bodily function without any psychic overtones — was ushered in. With it came a degree of promiscuity rarely witnessed throughout history. Then followed the acceptance and promotion of homosexuality under the great lesbian feminist leader, Kate Millett.

Kay Ebeling recalled a slogan of the consciousness-raising groups of the 1970s: "A woman without a man is like a fish without a bicycle."[12]

It was a sorry joke, with men and women moving farther and farther apart and sex separated from love, and feminists persuading women that it was their "right" to abdicate motherhood: let the state raise their children.

The truth is, moderate feminists, who may have brought about justified reforms — there *have* always been extreme injustices that should be addressed in every society —

were succeeded by radical feminists who orchestrated the feminist revolution from which we have suffered such dire results.

It was to become obvious that the revolution would eventually reach into almost every heart and home throughout the Western world: through divorce, one's own or that of loved ones; in deteriorating mental and physical health stemming from sexual liberation; in the lives of desperately troubled children. Radical feminist leaders would also introduce a socialist age, with a feminist-dominated economy and a totalitarianism utterly foreign to Western culture.

However, there is no doubt that by the 1990s men and women had begun to understand exactly what had been happening to them. They were recognizing the need to turn back the revolutionary tide by drawing together. *Together again*, reconciled, men and women can envision a far happier future; a future where love and sex can be brought *together again*; a future where mothers and children can be brought *together again*; a future where fathers and mothers and children can again stand firm as a family.

Saving the family, the proven bulwark of our Western nations in a past era, can become our crusade.

PART
I

Men and Women

Everybody knows that the boat is leaking.
Everyone knows the captain lied.
Everybody got this "broken" feeling —
Like their father or their dog just died.
Leonard Cohen

There is a brokenness throughout our society.
Jean Vanier, Founder of L'Arche Communities

The time is out of joint.
Hamlet

1

Coming Together to Talk: Disillusioned Women, Neutered Men

I do believe that the women of the Western world who had accepted feminist ideology as dictated by the radical feminist leaders during the past decades must now fully understand all its negative ramifications. It is their responsibility to initiate the changes and introduce the reforms that must come about if we are to restore justice and stability and healing to our troubled society — our "broken" society.

Bringing men and women together again — that will surely be seen as a priority. So many women, having found extreme disillusionment in their own lives, now set their sights on the truly greener pastures of reconciliation with the opposite sex. Leaving behind them all the old bitterness, the adamant distrust, the recriminations, they may begin to understand and even empathize with the plight of men, certainly the principal victims of the feminist revolution.

Replacing the so-called patriarchal society that, since time began, had taken into consideration the biological and psychological capabilities of men and women, with the present matriarchal society (in which all consideration of the biological and psychological capabilities of men and women are forbidden by law), seemingly placed men and women in two different time zones, with men most often deemed "the dinosaurs."

It is surprising that women of the Western world have taken almost three decades to realize and face up to the fact that it is *their* men — *their* probable boyfriends, *their* potential husbands, *their* fathers, *their* brothers and now, particularly, *their* sons — who have been left behind. The traditional male role is now undefined; it has been negated, and often is legally usurped, and its very future is uncertain.

As I watched four-year-old Maria on the teeter-totter, high in the air, her younger brother opposite and suddenly in peril, I rushed to balance them. I began to wonder if men and women can be persuaded to get off their teeter-totter, seeking deliberately such a simple "balance" on the way to reconciliation. At the same time, new healing attitudes could be struck to diffuse the mounting anger of men in their demands for a "level playing field." Few are denying that this is a legitimate demand; that men have been flagrantly handicapped.

When will women begin to *listen* to men again, to pause and once again show simple courtesy and even respect for their opinions? History has already recorded feminist censorship of male thought and the successful silencing of the male voice: the major factor in the rise of radical feminism. It was unfortunate that when women started shouting from the housetops, the confused male began to cower, seemingly unable to raise his voice, offering no defense.

In a world where we can pick up a telephone and talk to anyone in any corner of our universe; where instantaneous connections are made between states and nations;

where our voices are heard (even among the angels?) in outer space; where communication (as Marshall McLuhan, the famous Canadian educator, had predicted) has developed into the greatest influence in our lives and times — men and women simply stopped communicating. Even some feminists suggest that if men and women had continued to talk to each other in the early days of the Women's Liberation Movement, they might have been able to straighten out their differences *together*, reasonably attacking joint problems rather than each other.

Scholars today marvel that even the business leaders of North America were not able to make themselves heard. Feminist ideology translated into socialist ideology, insidiously pervading all areas of a free-enterprise, capitalistic system and eventually crippling North American commerce — which in the past had ensured economic growth and stability — through its interference in the marketplace.

It is ironic that by 1990, with the Eastern world turning its back on socialist principles and embracing freedom of the human spirit and justice in democratic principles, the feminist revolution in the Western world was moving the formerly "free-est" people on the face of the earth into the strictures of a socialist regime. The Marxist principles that ushered in the Communist era throughout the East would become acceptable throughout the West. These principles were:

- a return of women to the factories,
- the elimination of sex roles,
- the transformation of housekeeping into social industry,
- the communalization of child care,
- an "open" definition of the family,
- free and available divorce,
- unrestrained sexual freedom, and
- the elimination of the concept of illegitimacy.[1]

Although Britain and the United States are proving themselves slower in adopting all such socialist principles, Canada — a smaller country, with its population at a dwindling 27 million — has been manipulated by the most powerful of radical feminist leaders into accepting a socialism that, if not halted, can eventually sound the death knell of the traditional family lifestyle.

It is generally acknowledged that those radical feminist leaders have been able to achieve more in Canada than elsewhere, with the Canadian Charter of Rights and Freedoms guaranteeing the "right" of reverse discrimination against men and such feminist laws as pay equity (a cunningly devised term for equal pay for work of equal value) legislated and enforced in private as well as public sectors. Their crowning achievement was the election of the socialist New Democratic Party (NDP) government in the Province of Ontario in 1990, which brought one-third of the Canadian population under socialist rule.

Also in 1990, Judy Rebick, who had become a Marxist when she joined the Revolutionary Workers in college and later ran as an NDP in federal and provincial elections, would be hailed as the head of the feminist movement in Canada when she was elected president of the National Action Committee on the Status of Women (NAC),[2] the foremost federal lobby group (which, strangely, has received millions in funding from a federal Conservative government). An article in the June 1987 *World Marxist Review*, translated and distributed throughout the world, lauded the NAC for its "Communist" activities in achieving socialist goals.

While there is no doubt that feminist intimidation has known no bounds in the manipulation of politicians, particularly in Canada where it has been blatant and successful, its power in achieving a stranglehold on all media — television, radio, magazines, newspapers and publishing — has, I believe, been responsible for the Women's Liberation Movement's incredibly rapid advances. Censorship of all opposing views has been enforced as effectively as censorship by any militant dictatorship or Communist regime. Freedom of speech, enshrined in the constitutions of all democracies, has simply been ignored. As feminist ideology has flooded every area of communication in our culture, other voices questioning or opposing feminist ideology — voices that would have allowed the interplay of opposing views to seek and find truths — were successfully silenced.

Women were free to talk and write, and their books, such as those of Simone de Beauvoir, Germaine Greer and Kate Millett, would preach that

> the family, as that term is presently understood, must go . . . there is no biological reason why the two central functions of the family (socialization and reproduction) need be inseparable or even take place within it . . . The limited role allotted the female tends to arrest her at the level of biological experience. Therefore, nearly all that can be described as distinctly human rather than animal activity . . . is largely reserved for the male.[3]

Opposing voices were, until the late 1980s, rarely audible. Nicholas Davidson, in his book *The Failure of Feminism* (1988), considered the first and still the most comprehensive account of the Women's Liberation Movement in the Western world, explained:

> Expressing an opinion about gender was to guarantee swift and shrill assault . . . not so much because of the special opinion offered as because a "male" dared to offer an opinion at all. Poor shrimp! Didn't he realize that Feminism was Humanism?
> There is no hope . . . of men finding themselves

without respectful attention to the feminist insights. Men must assume a position of tutelage to women, deferring to their superior knowledge of human affairs. Because men's perceptions are clouded by the stultifying effects of masculinity, because men are desensitized by conditioning and rendered arrogant by inflated status, they need to relearn humility to the point of giving up their own masculine point of view.[4]

Any man who, in the earlier years, had dared to raise his voice, even in a mild manner in an academic setting, could also be threatened by physical assault. This was the case when Lionel Tiger, an internationally respected anthropologist, in a speech in Vancouver dared to question the extremely radical concepts in feminist ideology and was halted by serious bomb threats. Later, when a review of his book *Men in Groups* — a study of the importance of male bonding in the progress of world civilization — appeared in the national Canadian magazine *Maclean's*, feminists picketed the publishing house and copies of the magazine were subsequently withdrawn from the newsstands.[5] Courageous and undaunted, Lionel Tiger attempted a lecture series questioning feminist theory. The series began and ended in a packed amphitheater at McGill University in Montreal, where a Marxist-feminist leader, Marlene Dixon, succeeded in whipping a usually respectful and receptive audience of students into a dangerous mob of feminists, waving placards that read "Bullshit, Bullshit."[6]

When David Frost attempted to interview Lionel Tiger in New York, the author again appeared to be in physical danger from a stacked gallery of feminists cursing and shouting at both him and Frost. "Somebody had a copy of my book and it came whizzing at me," Tiger recalled. Such exhibitions intimidated and deterred other interviewers, particularly those who may have sought to be "fair" as well as controversial, from presenting anyone with opposing antifeminist views.[7] Tiger, in 1988, asked women "Are Men Redundant?" in an article of that title in the national Canadian women's magazine, *Chatelaine*. That article provides a mini-history of the feminist successes that, he believes, are leading directly to men's redundancy.[8]

Twenty years earlier, SCUM, the Society for Cutting Up Men, with branches across North America, had suggested in its manifesto:

> Men who are rational . . . won't kick or struggle or raise a distressing fuss, but will just sit back, relax, enjoy the show, and ride the waves to their demise.
>
> Life in this society being, at best, an utter bore and no aspect of society being at all relevant to women, there remains to civic-minded, responsible, thrill-seeking females only to overthrow the government . . . and destroy the male sex.
>
> The male . . . with his inability to relate and to feel compassion, has made of the world a shit-pile.[9]

Whipping up hate and vengeance against men in attacks similar to the one in the Montreal amphitheater — even attacks as bizarre as those in the SCUM *Manifesto* — would go unchallenged, with the power of feminists over media growing, imposing a veritable blackout on opposing opinions.

Ordinary women listening and learning from these tirades and unable to hear the voices of the other half of the population would suddenly decide to raise their own voices, in their own kitchens or places of employment, to the level of drowning out the voices of their men — their husbands, their boyfriends, their sons, their employers. "You are male chauvinist pigs — get out of my sight," became a slogan.

Men and women would indeed vanish from one another's sight once they no longer were able to talk things over. Today, lifting feminist censorship of the male voice, and of all opposing views, must be achieved if we are to restore balance and justice. Reuniting men and women — reconciliation — must depend on men and women being able to talk to each other again.

In the most shocking exhibition of feminist censorship, children are being indoctrinated in feminist theory from the very earliest grades. Dr. Paul Vitz, a professor of psychology at New York University, in a continent-wide study authorized by the U.S. Government's National Institute of Education, analyzed 90 school textbooks used by 60 to 88 percent of the children in the United States. His findings were nothing less than shocking.

For instance, "There is not one portrayal of a contemporary American family that clearly features traditional sex roles," Dr. Vitz said. The traditional family had been reduced to "people you live with," and nowhere in any texts were the words "marriage," "husband" or "homemaker" ever used. Women were invariably presented in the workplace, and there was nothing to suggest that "homemaking is an important job." *American parents, men or women, had never been consulted on such content.*

Dr. Vitz also regretted "the absence of any concern for non-material values . . . only money, status and enjoyment were presented as motivations for work, with no indication that many work out of concern for others, or because of the intrinsic value of certain kinds of work." Specific references to religion had been deliberately omitted. In the story of America's first Thanksgiving, the Pilgrim fathers were simply described as "people who make long trips."

"Are public school textbooks biased?" Dr. Vitz asks. "Are they censored? The answer to both is yes."[10]

Ignoring historical fact and all biological considerations, the most prolific publishing houses throughout North America came under feminist dominance by the early

1970s. McGraw-Hill issued an ultimatum to its editors in a 16-page booklet entitled "Guidelines for Equal Treatment of the Sexes in McGraw-Hill Company Publications," in which its editors were told:

> Women and girls should be portrayed as active partic-
> ipants in the same proportion as men and boys in
> stories, examples, problems, illustrations, discussion
> questions, test items, and exercises, regardless of sub-
> ject matter . . .
> Girls should be encouraged to show an interest in
> mathematics, mechanical skills, and active sports . . .
> Boys should be encouraged to develop an interest in
> poetry, art or music, or an aptitude for cooking,
> sewing or child care.[11]

There were words and terms that had to be censored out of all children's books once and for all, among them: housewife, lady, the girls, the fair sex, the better half, co-ed, the distaff side, authoress and poetess, plus all female-gender formations. How soon would dictionaries be forced to follow suit?

Laidlaw Brothers (a division of Doubleday) offered authors samples of sentences they could imitate, such as: "those girls learned karate" and "the astronaut had a physical before she returned to the base" and "her aunt scored a touchdown." The educational system as well as popular children's literature would be teaching children the new male role in society with such sentences as: "Gary will bake today" and "Dad mixed the ingredients" and "Chuck hung the curtains" and "the boys are in the sewing class."[12]

"My God," one usually nonprofane educator exploded — but in private — "our little girls are all supposed to grow up into tough old male-cloning robots, and our little boys, as sure as hell, are being conditioned into pansies." (I had to look up that old-fashioned word "pansy" in the dictionary, and found that it does not necessarily have a homosexual connotation but usually simply describes "an effeminate, ineffectual, simpering type of male.")

It was the international Macmillan publishing house that produced the most insidious guidelines in this area of denaturalization of our children. These commanded the firm's writers no longer to characterize women as "guardians of morality . . . peace-loving . . . above material concerns . . . compassionate . . . nurturers . . . self-sacrificing . . . modest . . . self-effacing . . . pure . . . innocent." The company was warning its writers that "binding young women with such demands can cripple them as severely as did binding their feet in old China."[13]

I never did believe that women could be so drastically denaturalized as these guidelines directed, but a book that appeared in the bookstores in January 1991 had a title that said it all: "Doesn't Anyone Blush Anymore?" The message of its author, Manis Friedman, certainly proved the enormous influence that such feminist indoctrination has had throughout the educational systems.[14]

I did hear Mike Anscombe, an anchor on Global Television, a national Canadian network, ask Gloria Steinem, founder and editor of *Ms*, "Why have Canadian feminists been able to achieve so much more than American feminists in the Women's Liberation Movement?" She answered, "I guess it's because American women are still too *lady-like.*" (The teenage girls in major North American cities who belong to gangs with names like the "Bangers" — and who have been convicted of more vicious crimes than teenage boys in similar gangs — must have received Gloria Steinem's message.)

Psychiatrists and psychologists throughout the Western world are now convinced that reverse stereotyping, often legislated irrevocably into our culture, is today posing the greatest danger to the mental health of future generations. They are claiming that deliberate steering and often forcing of little girls and little boys, at the earliest ages, away from their instinctive natures, denying them their natural aptitudes, may induce new and incurable forms of schizophrenia, with most serious consequences for the population as a whole.

Where were the voices of reason, of justice, of the male and female writers who must have seen the censorship throughout the publishing industry, particularly involving children's literature, as an unconscionable, almost criminal act denying freedom of thought and speech? It must have become obvious, even in the earliest days of the Women's Liberation Movement, that every major publishing house in the Western world had come under the control of radical feminists.

Professor Steven Goldberg's antifeminist arguments earned his book *The Inevitability of Patriarchy* the dubious honor of a citation in the 1988 *Guinness Book of World Records*, having received the greatest number of rejections — 69 from 55 publishers. However, when James Landis, a courageous editor at William Morrow, accepted and published the book, the publisher could look forward to breaking bestseller records.[15]

Nicholas Davidson laments the fact that book reviews in newspapers as prestigious as the *New York Times* up until the 1990s consistently promoted feminist ideology, as offered in any mediocre work, while ignoring or trashing any opposing work that had seen the light of day. "The *Times'* message on feminism has been especially effective because of the unusual degree of trust that most readers have in such a paper's reliability," he wrote.[16]

Rosemary Radford Reuther, who calls herself a "Catholic theologian," received unstinting praise in a *Times* review of her book, *Women-Church: Theology and Practice of Feminist Liturgical Communities*. In it she celebrates "a Ceremony for Abortion," and a "Coming-Out Rite for a Lesbian." The reviewer, Susan Schnur, a rabbi who teaches religion at

Colgate University in Hamilton, New York, gushed: "Over this next decade, the writing and rewriting of texts will be the homework for feminists in religion."[17]

Both prolific writers are proving leaders in the feminist revolution against the fundamental teachings of their own religions, while media continue to drown out opposing views, no matter how scholarly, whether in editorials or advertising. Meanwhile, in a 1990 spring issue of the *New York Times*, the paper ran a two-page advertisement for the movie *Nuns on the Run*, which was described as "the Funniest Anti-Clerical Transvestite Comedy of the Decade." In the same paper, a full-page advertisement praised the film *The Handmaid's Tale*, considered by many to be "bigoted and inflammatory" as well as pornographic in its depiction of sexual tyranny practiced by a religious fundamentalist society that mated superior "patriarchs" with young women who were forced to conceive and bear future generations.[18] That film was based on Canadian author and feminist activist Margaret Atwood's bestselling novel, which presented a terrifying interpretation of fundamentalism.

Where were the "good" people in the United States who may have insisted on censorship forbidding the National Endowment for the Arts (NEA), the government agency that takes $175 million of taxpayers' money every year, from funding exhibitions such as the one by Andres Serrano, which included a photo of Christ submerged in Serrano's urine? Or the one by David Wojinarowicz, which featured a photo of Christ shooting heroin and pictures of men performing perverted sex on each other and on animals? After all, "censorship" used to mean the control of material that threatened to corrupt and debauch mankind.[19]

Now, it often seems to mean the very opposite; for censorship silences material that questions perceived perversions in a society where antireligious, antimorality biases obviously abound.

Surely there can be no more blatant example of such censorship than that experienced by a renowned Canadian nun, Sister Lucille Durocher. Sister Lucille is the founder of Human Life International, Canada, a powerful arm of the Washington-based HLI, an organization founded by the world-famous theologian Father Paul Marx and dedicated to preserving "the family" and restoring moral values. When she dared to object to new directives published in a major 60-page report by the Catholic bishops of Quebec (formerly known as a bastion of Catholicism in the Western world), the sister was convicted of the so-called crime and given the enforced *sentence of silence* by her order. According to the report that she objected to, Catholicism should project

> the elimination of masculine and female stereotypes in church marriage documents; re-examine and theologically restate the perception of women and their role in the family and in marriage . . . Recognize that maternity does not define motherhood . . . Support feminism.[20]

Other bishops, among the millions across North America who support the sister's objections unreservedly, are expected to launch her appeal.

Michael Novak, who holds the George Frederick Jewett Chair at the American Enterprise Institute and is the publisher of *Crisis* magazine, writes:

> No one is consecrated as a bishop simply to bless the prejudices of his culture . . . A nation getting its moral education from Phil Donahue is not in good shape . . .
>
> One journalist wrote that the bishops are losing "credibility" on sexual issues, another that they are "losing the people in the pews." (This is self-delusion

. . . Catholic churches — and parking lots — are packed for Mass every Sunday.) Their plaintive advice to bishops was: conform.

But do these journalists really want the Catholic bishops to preach the same sexual ethic that rock videos, movies and magazines do? . . . to exhort our children to premarital intercourse at will, infidelity if desired, abortion on demand, and sexual preference ad libitum? Look around our culture now. Are people who hold such values happy?[21]

Decisions to follow society's mores rather than adhering steadfastly to the original tenets and practices that sustained troubled people in past ages were threatening the spiritual roots of other faiths as well. The United Church, the largest Protestant denomination in Canada, was seen by many to be disintegrating as a result of recent policies: God was designated simply a "presence" — more often a "She" than a "He," and, under the influence of homosexual activists, the hierarchy sanctioned the ordination of homosexuals — who could become the role models for susceptible youths.

At the same time, Jewish feminist writers have been denouncing all doctrines pertaining to women in Hebrew custom, suggesting alternatives that would unravel the very tapestry of a faith historically magnificent in its survival through centuries of persecution.

The book *Ritual Slaughter*, by Sharon Drache, published in Canada and funded by the federal government, horrified readers with descriptions of the wretchedly oppressed, male-dominated lives of the women of the Hasidic sect. It was certainly responsible for one young Christian woman I know breaking off her engagement to her Jewish fiance.

Hasidism, acknowledged to be the most fundamental branch of Judaism, was founded in southern Poland in the 18th century, with the most joyous, highly emotional rites designed to lift the spirits of the Jewish people in the poverty-stricken ghettos of Eastern Europe. It was recognized as a modern voice in Israel, with members of the Hasidic sect elected to Parliament in 1988. While many Jews express concern at Hasidic rigidity today, such books as *Ritual Slaughter* are simply seen as feminist fictionalized attacks on Jewish males, using "subjugation" of women generally to further the case against men.[22]

Rabbi Immanuel Schochet in a newspaper interview claimed that Jews do not have to apologize for the status of women in Judaism; that their revered status is at the very heart of the faith, and is "celebrated throughout our services"; that in the very beginning, "When God gave the people the Torah, He told Moses,'Go first to the women, and if they accept it, I know that the Jewish people will be preserved.'" Rabbi Schochet believes that feminists today who create new texts to change Jewish laws and customs are simply "reducing religion to an ego trip."[23]

R. D. Kernohan, former editor of the Church of Scotland's journal, *Life and Work*, says: "The Western churches want to be relevant . . . They say they 'must listen to what people are saying' . . . but in listening so much they can find themselves stammering spiritually, when they need to speak. In trying to relate to the secular they risk being secularized themselves."[24]

The voices of the greatest orators preaching fundamentalist truths have always been heard. Dr. Robert Schuller's services from the Crystal Cathedral are carried on 31 television networks throughout the world, Billy Graham talks to multitudes in his personal appearances throughout the world, and Rabbi Manis Friedman's worldwide lectures and videos reverberate throughout all religious communities. However, other scholarly male voices that may have attempted to bring reason and balance into all secular areas of society were deliberately drowned out by the voices of the "mugwumps" and the converted, whose accomplishments were consistently blown out of all proportion in feminist-controlled media. (The word "mugwumps" was coined by John Diefenbaker, known as the most colorful of all Canadian prime ministers, to describe those politicians for whom he had little respect, allies or opponents, who would "straddle the fence — their mug on one side and their wump on the other."[25])

The earnest mugwumps were wearing the hair shirts from the very beginning of the Women's Liberation Movement. However, while they seemed to be manfully shouldering all the blame the feminists heaped upon them by abjectly apologizing for all their so-called sins and omissions, they also insisted that men did have some worthwhile attributes that contributed to society, justifying their place in a feminist culture.

Introducing a collection of articles in the book *Beyond Patriarchy: Essays by Men on Pleasure, Power, and Change*, Michael Kaufman, the editor, explained: "Each contributor is attempting to crack his own armor and challenge his oppressive relations with women and other men"; but he was also compelled to add that men were not "altogether rotten." He wrote:

> While we are very critical of the overall shape of masculinity in today's society, we want to affirm the many qualities associated with masculinity that are within every human being's range of possibilities: our sexual desire, our physical and emotional strength, our ability to operate under pressure, our courage, our creativity, and intellect, our dedication to a task, self-sacrifice and so on.[26]

In 1975, Warren Farrell's *The Liberated Man* was a bestselling book among women. He pleased them by urging his own sex to "get beyond condescension and contempt for women; to stop dominating them"; but his most important message was that a man "must get in touch with the feminine parts of his own personality." One critic called this a "wimp's surrender," and the author himself admitted that the book had met an extremely negative response from men.[27]

Farrell's book *Why Men Are the Way They Are*, which followed in 1986, included a chapter entitled "What I Love Most About Men," in which he listed admirable male characteristics, among them: the fact that they are self-starters; that they have great control of their emotions during crisis; that they accept responsibility, and risks. Another chapter compared female chauvinism with male chauvinism, as well as discussing unfair female attacks on men. Feminists were mortified to learn that the author had moved back into the male camp.[28]

The truly converted males are known to gather in small groups in Britain and the United States and Canada to bolster their resolve in being the "New Men." One small group in Canada gained wide publicity when it received a federal government grant, with its very name, "New Men, Partners in Change," signifying the "new order." Meeting regularly, they struggle to "overcome their sexism, their conditioning, their stereotyping."

The founder and leader of the group, Kenneth Fisher, a divorced father of teenage sons, admitted in a newspaper interview that he was still carrying the wounds and guilt from a failed marriage, although he was now happily married to a woman he met through the companion-wanted columns of an Ottawa weekly. He is convinced he has been instrumental in starting a "men's cultural revolution." He expounded:

. . . its primary purpose is to open up men to their feelings . . . The price of masculinity is growing up deprived of emotion and feeling. We're denying half of our house, and that half of our house haunts us.

We're manipulated by our fear of feeling.

"New Men" don't have to shoulder the burdens alone, they can share power, change jobs, take time to get to know their children, be themselves — and in the process they will feel better. There will be fewer heart attacks, less hypertension, less alcoholism, and more pleasure in life, as men learn what it is to be human.[29]

Such neutered voices were welcomed in all feminist media outlets, while the voices that might have questioned the arrogance of feminist males in suggesting that man had never been "human" were muted.

The first honest and sincere attempt to start serious dialogue again between the sexes, with men at last allowed to express their opinions in print, may have been in the publishing of the 1987 book *Men in Feminism*. It was a collection of 20 articles by world-renowned academics, such as Jacques Derrida, celebrated contemporary philosopher; Nancy Miller, professor of women's studies at New York's Barnard College; Terry Eagleton, Oxford fellow and general editor of Blackwell's *Rereading Literature* series; Meaghan Morris, lecturer and film critic in Australia; and Cary Nelson, professor of English at the University of Illinois.

Men in Feminism was inspired, according to the editors Alice Jardine (associate professor of languages at Harvard) and Paul Smith (associate professor of cultural studies at Carnegie Mellon University), by an article in the *Dalhousie Review*. Written by Stephen Heath, a fellow at Jesus College, Cambridge, that article expressed in no uncertain terms a man's refusal to accept feminist ideology:

Men's relation to feminism is an impossible one. This is not said sadly, nor angrily (though sadness and anger are both known and common reactions) . . .

which does not mean, of course not, that I can do nothing in my life, that no actions are open to me, that I cannot respond . . . It just means that I have to realize nevertheless — and this is an effort not a platitude — that I am not where they are and that I cannot pretend to be . . . which is the impossibility of my, men's relation.[30]

Unfortunately, anger was certainly a common factor in the majority of the *Men in Feminism* articles. Professor Denis Donaghue was quoted as regretting: "It may be the case . . . the best a man can do is keep out of their [women's] way." Yet later he wondered if "appeasing the anger" in dialogue could lead to understanding and an armistice between men and women. He recalled:

At the end of the Oresteia, the avenging Furies have been transformed into the benign Eumenides, a change of disposition that authorities . . . (our institutions of politics and sociology) . . . can bring about by observing the propriety of discourse. Nothing as fundamental as a change of heart is required."[31]

Any hope of transforming the Furies of the feminist revolution into the kindly goddesses in the old Greek plays was, however, dispelled by the female writers. While the male writers in the book analyzed feminism as a bleak, uncompromising philosophy daring to trifle with nature in the destruction of men, the majority of the female writers in the collection continued to rail at all men for their lack of sensitivity and their blindness in refusing to accept all feminist tenets. Words were being thrown across the field, but they would fall like stones.

Still, men were being allowed to "talk back," at last. Before the very dams broke, enlightened social engineering was beginning to seek new directions for the troubled waters. By 1990, the intense longing of men and women for reconciliation, for healing, for companionship, for meaningful relationships, for the understanding that could come about only through communications, from talking to one another again — such longing was certainly springing from the very hearts of men and women throughout the Western world. The wellspring of reconciliation would come to be recognized in a great new surge of the human "spirit."

In 1990, Barbara Reynolds, *USA Today's* Inquiry editor, was denouncing such publications as the *New York Times*, the *Washington Post* and *Newsweek* for censoring "the spirit," "the soul," from Czech President Vaclav Havel's New Year's Day address, in deleting his key words "Jesus" and the "Christian spirit" and his declaration of his country's role as "the spiritual crossroads of Europe."

In the same article, the writer told the story of the Reverend Laszlo Tokes, the Hungarian pastor "who sparked the Romanian revolution" and was saved from execution only the day before the tyrant Nicolai Ceausescu was overthrown. Tokes now preaches that "Eastern Europe is not just in a political revolution but a religious renaissance."[32] Furthermore, men and women are not apart throughout the Eastern world. Together, they survive.

Bringing men and women together again with new understanding and reconciliation throughout our Western world may promise a similar renaissance.

2
Hoodwinking Women: The First False Premise

My mother, who often likes to reduce all the major problems in life into the simplest of explanations, said: "If only the women had not been so gullible, they might have taken Betty Friedan with a grain of salt, as well as all the radical feminists who followed her, sorting out some good from the bad, rather than plunging ahead, hoodwinked, into the millions of problems we face today."

She saw the Women's Liberation Movement simply as a "pack of lies, misconceptions, utterly false premises" that seduced a whole society. Furthermore, she accused the protagonists of knowingly leading a "flock of sheep to their slaughter," simply in a power struggle to achieve their own revolutionary goals. (My mother, who lives on a farm, has never been one to mince her words.)

Of course, Betty Friedan must be held responsible for the first false premise of the Women's Liberation Movement, a premise that would succeed in denigrating a woman's former traditional role in marriage, motherhood and homemaking. In her book *The Feminine Mystique*, pub-

lished in 1963, women were told that they could achieve
self-fulfillment and reach their full potential as "persons"
only in a solitary search for their own "identity," in their
own individual goals, in work always outside the home —
"liberated" from all biological considerations — "liberated"
from husbands and children and homes — "liberated"
from *all the needs of others*. She wrote:

> There are aspects of the housewife role that make it
> almost impossible for a woman of adult intelligence
> to retain a sense of human identity . . . women of
> ability . . . who grow up wanting to be "just a house-
> wife," are in as much danger as the millions who
> walked to their own death in the concentration
> camps.
>
> The prisoners were forced to adopt childlike be-
> haviour . . . merge themselves into an amorphous
> mass . . . in work which produced great fatigue . . .
> required no mental concentration . . . was sometimes
> senseless and was controlled by the needs of others.[1]

It was true that in the early years of the Women's Liberation Movement many homemakers (and I was one of
them) were able to give short shrift to such wildly imagina-
tive rhetoric, never questioning their own self-fulfillment,
their own "identity" found in commitments to marriage and
motherhood and lifestyles principally concerned with "the
needs of others." (We knew intuitively what Albert
Schweitzer expressed: "There is not one happy person on
the face of this earth who has not learned to serve
others.")

Happiness and other immeasurable rewards were at-
tainable in the goals of such homemakers, and they would
read in disbelief that their lifestyles could be
"monotonous," not requiring "mental concentration," and
that they would receive no "recognition." They *knew* that

nurturing children and making and keeping a marriage wonderfully viable could be the most challenging, the most complex and difficult work in the world, demanding considerable intellect and far greater skills, indeed, than most women would ever require in their one-dimensional workplace jobs.

Personally, in denying Friedan's feminist lies, I was able to draw on my own experiences. I had left a prestigious, lucrative position as an editor of a national magazine for a much more important career: that of a homemaker and mother. Neither then nor since have I ever had the slightest doubt that the work of a homemaker-mother can be the most important work in the world, of the greatest value in ensuring a stable society. I believe this conviction may be proven now in the sorry results of the abandonment of the homemaker-mother role by so many women during the feminist era. Those who wantonly abandoned the role, those persuaded or cajoled into being a part of the "me generation" — these women can only imagine the rewards.

Homemaking in itself, including cooking, always was considered a creative art form. How could one not have respect for the good cook? Didn't chefs pull down some of the fattest salaries?

At the grass-roots level, here was the crux of the matter. A woman working as a chef in a restaurant or hotel, pulling down that salary, had found her "identity" and self-fulfillment, and she was to be respected. Conversely, the homemaker-mother, in her vitally important, many-faceted career, drawing on all her resources — mental, psychological and physical, day and night, responsible for the well-being, the physical and psychological health of all members of her family — would never count her self-fulfillment and her immeasurable rewards in dollars and cents. Thus, she would be reviled as a "houseslug."

The concept was so ludicrous to many women that, in

those earliest years of the movement, they simply failed to pay any attention. Ruth R. Wisse, a professor of Yiddish literature at McGill University in Montreal, was one of these women. In a major *Commentary* magazine article that appeared in 1988 and was subsequently condensed in *Reader's Digest*, she wrote: "Convinced that women were the practical gender, I was sure they would never be deceived by false ideology, and I expected the Movement to evaporate as quickly as it had materialized. It was the worst cultural prediction of my life."[2]

Gentle voices, rarely allowed media space, would be heard from time to time, attempting to neutralize that first false premise, but to no avail. One homemother, Janet Scott Barlow, obviously devastated as feminism continued to erode all respect for her priorities, spoke out in an article in the prestigious *Commonweal* magazine:

> A woman who can help to instil in her growing children compassion and courage and honor and humor, while also managing housework and homework and carpools and illness, and do it all every day, year after year, is a woman who *knows* something. Things being what they are, she is also a woman who needs to be *told* that she knows something.
>
> Mothers needed to hear aloud a truth that existed in their own minds and hearts, but seemed to exist in few other places: that the commonplace work of raising children had value — not dollar value, but social value, personal value, moral value . . . that all human endeavor has a cost . . .
>
> Women were told that they were suppressing their *selves* and living through their children . . . They knew it was a *lie*.
>
> The essence of being a mother is woman's awareness that for as long as she lives, she will be bound to her children by her own intimate love and concern

and hope. Some of the by-products of this awareness are human insight, philosophical and psychological resilience, and the instinct to know what's important and what isn't . . .
The large nuggets of genuine reward and satisfaction [can be] found nowhere else in life . . .
. . . I have followed my nature, my needs, and my personal commitment, and have remained a fulltime mother . . . "Fulltime" meaning all the work, all the care, all the time (with help from my husband after his day at his fulltime job). Fulltime in spite of the fact that my household could have used a second income.[3]

What household could not use a second income one way or another? Feminist revolutionary leaders quickly realized that there were some women who could not be driven out of their homes, freed of all the needs of husbands and children, by contempt or ridicule and finally peer pressure; but they could be persuaded through all the monetary advantages of a two-career lifestyle.

By 1990, feminists were preaching that most women "must work," that families today could not survive on one income — another blatant falsehood — although many families having moved into much larger houses have those mortgages that seem to require two incomes. Hundreds of studies have shown that middle-class women do spend that second income on mortgages for larger homes, as well as on transportation, the second car, exotic holidays, restaurant meals, prepared food and day care.

Dan Seligman, in his column "Keeping Up" in *Fortune*, February 15, 1988, argued that American families were really under no more economic pressure to generate two incomes in the 1980s than they were in the 1950s. He admitted that women today were certainly under new social pressures to engage in careers outside the home, and that they had a wide range of job opportunities that were not

available to women 30 years ago. However, he claimed, a
father in the 1980s, on average, was better able to support
his family than was a father in the 1950s. In 1950, the sole-
supporting head of the family was earning $4833, which,
adjusted to the inflation rate over the past 30 years, would
approximate $22,000. The corresponding earnings of the
average sole-supporting father in 1986 was $25,803.[4]
Economic study after study confirms the findings in the
Fortune article. The daddies in the 1990s will be able to
support those mommies who wish to stay home — if not
wickedly burdened in taxation to fund the early schooling
(estimated to cost billions) and the day care demanded by
other families.

Today, the teachings of Lenin are falling into disrepute
throughout the Soviet Union; why, then, should the socialist goals in feminist ideology — notably, Universal Day
Care — not be discredited throughout the Western world
as well? "Unless women are brought to take an indepen-
dent part not only in political life generally, but also in daily and universal public service," Lenin stated, "it is no use
talking about socialism."

In 1920, following the Russian Revolution, Lenin was
calling for "a revolution in sexual relations" that would end
"the decay, putrescence, and filth of bourgeois marriage,
with its difficult dissolution." This demand was directly responsible for the Comintern, in 1924, eliminating state
recognition of family commitments and legalizing abortion
and easy divorce, and was ultimately responsible for much
of the social malaise in the Soviet Union today.[5]

How ironic that, in 1989, on International World Wom-
en's Day, feminist revolutionaries throughout the Western
world were parading through the downtown streets of all
major cities, celebrating Lenin's socialist principles by
chanting slogans and carrying placards damning our Western democratic capitalistic system. And in the very same
month of the very same year a woman in Russia, Vitaly

Korotich, editor of the Soviet weekly, *Ogonyok*, was writing: "We must fight that women have the right to stay home . . . if they so wish."[6] In November 1990, a Soviet poll showed that one in five Soviet women were already determined to stay home to care for their families. (Restoring social esteem to family values and commitments was actually under way in Russia with the 1936 and 1941 amendments to Lenin's divorce and abortion laws.)

It is surely ironic that women's organizations dedicated to preserving the family, such as the Eagle Forum in the United States and REAL WOMEN in Canada, are now seen as fighting alongside Vitaly Korotich for women to be allowed "choices" — including "the right to stay home . . . if they so wish."

Feminist socialism in the Western world would withdraw that "right," forcing women to work outside the home: through taxation, to pay for universal or partially funded day care; through affirmative action and quota systems, which arbitrarily take jobs away from sole-supporting husbands to give to women; and through pay equity (equal pay for work of equal value), which denies sole-supporting husbands their justified raises while often unjustly raising the pay of women (who, according to all statistics, work 30 percent fewer weekly hours than men do).

Betty Friedan herself had actually fought against socialism in the National Organization of Women (NOW), the organization she founded in the United States, defeating the powerful Young Socialist Alliance (YSA), a branch of the Socialist Workers' Party. This party would have taken a more direct route toward a socialist system.

In Canada, however, socialist forces in the National Action Committee on the Status of Women (NAC) certainly dominated the direction of the Women's Liberation Movement from the very beginning, under the influence of such powerful member groups as the Women's Commission of the Communist Party of Canada and under such leaders as Paula Fletcher (onetime chairman of the Manitoba Communist Party) and Judy Rebick (onetime Marxist member of the Revolutionary Workers, who became president of NAC in 1990).[7]

Committed to such feminist socialist principles as Universal Day Care, feminists throughout North America are still seen as simply dusting off Lenin's prerogatives, among them ridding the state of what he had called the "bourgeois" marriage, in order to mold a people into a more easily controlled amorphous mass.

In the Western world, the traditional family lifestyle, based as it is on family members taking care of one another, would take a direct hit from the first false premise in the feminist revolution. Introduced as a cornerstone of the movement by Betty Friedan (who, I believe, was superimposing her own frustrations and failures, her own disenchantment with marriage and family lifestyle, on generations of other women), this false premise — "liberation" through the renouncing of all former responsibilities, of commitment to the loving care of spouse and children — denigrated the role of homemother.

Betty Friedan was the Pied Piper, and within a few years middle-class women across the continent were streaming after her, freeing themselves from all family ties and setting forth on a new, hedonistic drive toward self-fulfillment that would soon countenance divorce.

With women initiating divorce in more than 75-90 percent of all cases, according to statistics that remain constant, the disintegration of the North American family was under way. Later, the sexual liberation of women, introduced into the Women's Liberation Movement by such writers as Germaine Greer and Shulamith Firestone, would encourage infidelity and promiscuity, accelerating divorce and the disintegration of families.

The bewilderment of men, generally, in those early

years, as strident women brushed past them, was voiced by *New York Times* columnist Leonard Kreigel. In a television interview, he claimed that men had lost "their structure, their definition, their purpose in a feminist world."[8]

Anita Gradin, Sweden's international trade minister, accompanying the king and queen of Sweden on an official visit to the United States in 1988, expressed her concern at the plight of men in a transitional society. She had earlier authorized a comprehensive study of 5000 men in Sweden, and what came back to her, she said, was "a collective scream for help." Indeed, she was suggesting government assistance in establishing courses "to teach men some new role"! In Sweden, however, bringing men and women together again may be a lost cause.[9]

Socialist Sweden, with every feminist tenet in place, is now seen by many as a dying nation. Of Sweden's 8.3 million people, 3.1 million live alone; there are no choices and no options; men and women work outside the home, with 70 percent of men's wages and 45 percent of women's garnered in taxes. In Sweden one finds nationalized child care, open sex, very few marriages, little religion, a shrinking birth rate and the highest suicide rate in the world. In 1984, in the Stockholm area alone, a distress hotline received 95,000 telephone calls threatening suicide.[10]

Swedish people, among them Anita Gradin, admit that they are an unhappy population, with little hope of dislodging socialism. And this is the sort of socialism that feminist philosophy would establish in the Western world, the socialism without choices.

The first false premise of the Women's Liberation Movement denied intelligent women a choice, and feminist leaders today tirelessly fight for, and achieve, legislation — unfair taxation for one-career families, affirmative action and pay equity — that still denies all women a choice, that still drives them away from their husbands and relieves them of the family responsibilities that many women throughout the Western world now yearn for more than anything else on earth.

Of course, there are all those marvelously talented women, often with rare and unusual skills, who always have been and always will be working outside the home, leaving nannies or loving relatives to substitute as mothers of their children. Only about 18 percent of all mothers working outside the home hold executive positions in industry or are prominent in the professions. It seems ironic that many of these women who have reached such echelons of power and prestige are the very mothers who are leading the exodus of women from the workplace back to the home. Many studies similar to the one conducted at Lowell University confirm this trend.

Then there are those women who truly do not like children and have no wish to include children in their lifestyles. While a woman's aversion to raising children may have seemed unnatural in a former culture, women in a feminist era believe that refusing to have children is a perfectly legitimate choice. A surprising number of young university women, according to surveys, have decided to make that choice.

There have always been approximately 20 percent of all mothers who indeed must work to support their families, owing to innumerable circumstances beyond their control. Many of these women seem to have very special abilities in gaining the understanding and support and devotion of wonderful children. A social worker told me: "There are no stupid children. Instinctively they know if they are wantonly abandoned, or if a mother works for their welfare." As for the single mothers, who compose the fastest growing segment of the population over the past 10 years, they must be unreservedly supported by a society that may be seen as directly responsible for those numbers, in its endorsement of the "single cult" and single parenthood as taught in feminist ideology.

Hoodwinking women into believing that any of their efforts on this earth could be more important than the nurturing care of their own children may be seen as the most evil and far-reaching achievement of the Women's Liberation Movement. That first false premise must be denied.

In the 1990s, women throughout the Western world, wherever they are, at home or in the workplace, are beginning to understand that children and husbands and families symbolize what life itself is all about. The majority of them no longer want to be "liberated" from their children and their husbands, their families.

They are finding joy in readjusting their priorities — toward that far happier future.

3
Toppling Patriarchy: The Second False Premise

In the women's studies programs offered in all North American universities, the second false premise of the Women's Liberation Movement has been the primary theme: that men have been oppressing women from the beginning of time, and modern men must now pay and pay for their forefathers' and their own sins of oppression.

Driving a large percentage of women toward their new self-fulfilling goals, separating them from their homes and their husbands and their children, was accomplished — under the first false premise — by Betty Friedan and the radical feminists who followed her. However, feminist protagonists soon realized that the rise and ultimate dominance of feminism could be achieved only by turning the whole weight of the movement into discrediting men by tying the traditional male role to biological and psychological motives. Feminism, rising on the backs of men, could, the movement's leaders determined, soon topple the so-called patriarchy of the past.

It was then that men throughout the Western world

were relentlessly charged, condemned and sentenced, without any opportunity for defense, as the "oppressors" of women. Women, the feminists declared, had been subjected to multitudes of injustices throughout the ages. Yet it can be demonstrated historically that the so-called evils in patriarchy were seldom conceived by chauvinistic design. And, as a most important step in our efforts to bring about reconciliation between the sexes, we must study history to deny this second false premise in the Women's Liberation Movement.

Historically, men and women adopted specific roles as a result of evolutionary events. The deliberate discrimination attributed to a former patriarchy was simply invented by modern feminists, who, for example, would have us believe that former prime minister Benazir Bhutto of Pakistan was the "first woman to head an Islamic country." (The historical fact is that Jalalat-ad-din Raziya ruled Delhi during the 13th century AD.)

In ancient eras, men and women rose alike — in state and family affairs — according to their birth or talents. As far back as the second millennium BC, female pharaohs such as Hapshepset ruled Egypt. Cleopatra, of course, was to become the most famous of the queens of Egypt a thousand years later. And Boadicea, queen of what is now Norfolk in England, rose after the downfall of her husband to lead the East Anglians in turning back the Roman legions in 61 AD and today is revered as one of the greatest warriors of all times.

Contrary to modern feminist literature, women have always owned large areas of land in their own names. Throughout the centuries land and wealth were inherited by daughters from their fathers and by wives from their husbands. Many of the greatest religious communities throughout Europe were established by powerful abbesses who had inherited great family wealth.

The English custom of the eldest son falling heir to the

family title and estate, particularly damned by the feminists as unacceptable discrimination against daughters, simply evolved as a rational solution to the problem of choice, with its arbitrary pitfalls, and was considered a far preferable custom than drawing a child's name from among many *in a hat.* Custom became a tradition.

The new expectations and attitudes regarding male and female roles, which led to the so-called evils in a patriarchy that feminist ideology has focused on, actually evolved during the 18th and 19th centuries in Europe, when the industrial age with all its new technology was transforming the lives of men and women.

When wood, water and wind were replaced by steam, it would prove as great a phenomenon in that era as nuclear power has proven in our era. The introduction of steamboats and steam engines was accompanied by the feverish building of canals and railways and roads. With the invention of the flying shuttle and the power loom, the greatest textile industry in the world was born. Meanwhile, new methods of coal mining and iron production were vital in other manufacturing. Factories sprang up in every corner of Britain, and British trade carried industrialization east and west. (The United States would not become truly industrialized until after the Civil War of 1861-65. French industrialization lagged far behind in those years, with France racked in revolution.)

The British amassed great fortunes, and, as seen in census figures of the period, an enormous middle class evolved. Such fortunes were never in the hands of the aristocrats, who would remain rooted in agriculture on their land holdings.

The separation of the sexes that took place among the largest proportion of the population was a direct result of the rising fortunes of that middle class, and it certainly was never seen then as a separation. Men had simply flocked into the factories and trade centers, leaving their womenfolk to tend the family homes and farms, to raise the children and to care for the communities.

These middle-class women, as their circumstances were enhanced, adopted new manners and customs as full-time *chatelaines*. At the same time, the middle-class men returning to their homes each evening may have imagined themselves as the lords and barons of old — returning from conquests to their own "castles." Their homes and families became increasingly the source of all comforts and joys, and it was then that the husband appeared to take on the new mantle of "head" of the home and family, with all the responsibilities of a sole protector and provider. The family "team" was seen as consisting of such a titular "head," with the wife revered as the homemaker. Responsible not only for a well-ordered household but also for the psychological and physical well-being of all members of her family, the wife was placed on a pedestal by society.

Furthermore, in a majority of families the wife administered the family funds. The North American farm wife continues to do so, and, although we are led to assume that modern spouses all keep separate bank accounts, statistics record that 66 percent of all household checks are written by women. "Male chauvinist pigs" in a patriarchy had oppressed women particularly in the control of the purse strings, feminists have tried to make us believe. Historical fact, right up to recent studies, has shown quite the opposite.

In the early years, only a woman who had been widowed or whose husband's wages could not support the family would work outside the home. The safety and welfare generally of such women were the constant concern of many renowned reformers, such as Lord Anthony Shaftesbury, whose efforts to get women out of the mines and other traditionally dangerous occupations matched Charles Dickens' determination for reform in the employment of children. All women would be "biologically handicapped," in the opinion of these reformers, for any such employment. All women were to be protected and respected: they were "the mothers of our race."

Actually, feminist leaders throughout the Western world have been seen as relentless battering rams, brainwashing a society into believing that all men have been patriarchal monsters, oppressors of women, discriminators against women from the beginning of time. Of course, anyone can point to numerous cases of unjustified discrimination in every era. Surely, however, we must be ready to admit honestly that very few instances were not as the result of biological considerations or of the psychological aspirations of women generally.

Women, until the onslaught of the feminist revolution in 1963, certainly aspired to the traditional family lifestyle with all its dignity and stability and strengths that developed in the wake of the Industrial Age. It was only then that they were persuaded that the "me-first" goals — with a socialist state accepting family responsibilities — would be more desirable.

My husband's grandmother and her sister graduated from the University of Toronto in 1904, and their two best friends were women doctors. Eventually they were all happily married, the two doctors practicing out of their homes. Great-Aunt Maud had a magnificent life, settling in the Peace River district of northern Alberta, where she raised her children, helped her husband in the only drugstore in a vast area, helped as well in the farming of a huge tract of broom, and still had time to found not only a hospital, but also a drama league that would win innumerable national awards.

Their contemporaries who, in the majority of cases, did not seek higher education simply "chose" earlier marriages, with sole ambitions to be "perfect" mothers and "helpmeets." It would seem that the majority of them also had the staying power to become "perfect" mothers. Being a "helpmeet" (a respected word that feminists eliminated from modern language) could mean their support in stores, in farms and in any other family team enterprise. My mother says: "I didn't need a Liberal Arts degree either. I read right through the Harvard classics (20 tomes are still on her shelves), as well as all of Charles Dickens, while nursing my babies!" And, of course, she has never stopped reading, and happens to be the wisest woman I know.

Older women generally cannot see "discrimination of women by men" as set out in feminist ideology. To begin, very few would ignore all biological considerations that have dictated the male and female roles throughout history. Furthermore, they can cite hundreds of examples of women with particular ambitions who, with dogged determination and dedication and great talent and skills, have reached the heights to which they aspired. There have always been the Margaret Thatchers and Golda Meiers and Rebecca Lees. (Rebecca Lee in 1864 "became the first black woman to receive a medical degree, from the New England Female Medical College in Boston," becoming legend in all black and white communities.[1])

The *Encyclopaedia Britannica*, 1962 edition, published one year *before* the onslaught of the Women's Liberation Movement, recorded that women did not face any limitations where public office or property rights were concerned:

Women hold the most exalted public offices. They have been governors of several states, members of the United States Senate and House of Representatives, members of the president's cabinet and judges in both the federal courts and the courts of many of the states. Indeed there is no legal obstacle to the election of a woman as president or vice president of the United States.[2]

Feminists are so determined in insisting that the so-called male oppression and discrimination of the past justify the most punitive female reverse discrimination today that they would simply remove the men, or block the men, to legislate women into all echelons of power, notably politics. What the feminists refuse to admit, however, is that the majority of women do not wish to seek political office with its grinding demands. At an 1988 all-parties women's conference in Canada's capital, which specifically sought out female candidates, not one Canadian woman agreed to throw her hat into the ring. Canadian women also refused to consider an all-feminist party, as suggested in an inspiring address by Kristen Halldorstotter, who explained how her Women's Alliance Party was gaining ground in Iceland. Still, government-funded feminist councils would press on to force a 50 percent representation of women in Parliament by 1994. In 1989, Pat Carney, retiring from a cabinet position, was tendered a going-away gift of $1 million for projects to attract women into politics.[3]

In exasperation, Mildred Istona, editor of *Chatelaine*, Canada's premier magazine for women, in her April 1989 editorial wrote:

> It baffles me that some women persist in rationalizing our less than proportional representation in Ottawa by making excuses. How often have we heard the litany of complaints: that women do not have enough money, that we don't get adequate party support, that we are used as sacrificial lambs in no-win ridings? And how often have women of all political stripes flown in the face of these excuses and emerged triumphant? The same victim mentality stirs paranoia about new technology . . . and free trade . . .
>
> Lately, women have even taken to blaming other women for their reluctance to vote for their own sex. When will we face up to the fact that women, like

men, are not a monolith and we do not vote as a bloc . . .
Let's stop making excuses and let's start facing facts. The real reason women do not have proportional representation in this country's government is that not enough of us seek nomination and because family priorities still override personal ambition in most of our minds.

Anne Johnston, a Toronto councillor, and a defeated federal and mayoral candidate, told a meeting of women that her marriage had broken up because of her involvement in politics. "No one has ever done a study of women politicians, but I bet most of them don't have children, and I bet that most of them don't like to leave town . . . Women unconsciously put the family first," she was convinced.[4]

Denouncing "professional feminists who have whined and wailed and hidden behind *discrimination* . . . perpetuating the myth that females are second-class citizens," Maureen Sabia, a prominent lawyer and director of numerous Canadian and international corporations, has told women: "We have seen the enemy — and she is *us*."[5]

Margot Furk, a British Columbian chartered accountant who was a delegate at a national Progressive Conservative party convention in Montreal, had similar views. Columnist Hugh Winsor wrote that "she had the ability and capability to go wherever she wanted to go and did not want special treatment from the government or anyone else . . ." But Furk believes that affirmative action is a socialist policy that does not belong in any Conservative party.[6]

I am convinced that the majority of ordinary citizens throughout the Western world are today wondering how we could have been conned into accepting the many outright lies as well as half-truths concerning past male discrimination that have led to affirmative action programs, among other injustices, now legislated against men in our society. A prominent member of the New Jersey legislature has been quoted as remarking: "I can't imagine why we were unable to see through to the revolutionary motives of most of the radical feminist leaders, who have admitted they are socialists, or lesbian — so often out of touch with the other half of the population, or are simply power-seekers. We might have stopped them — before a whole generation of men became casualties."

Golda Meier was one world leader who was frank in her appraisal of feminists:

> . . . those crazy women who . . . go around all di-sheveled and hate men? They're crazy, crazy. But how can one accept such crazy women who think it's a misfortune to get pregnant and a disaster to bring children into the world? And when it's the greatest privilege we women have over men!
>
> When I joined the Zionist Labor Movement — ninety percent of my comrades were men. I've lived and worked with men all my life, and yet to me the fact of being a woman has never, never I say, been an obstacle. It's never made me uncomfortable or giv-en me an inferiority complex. Men have been good to me.[7]

The truth is that Golda Meier's "crazies" have been able to accomplish appalling feats, particularly in Canada, where they are acknowledged to have been more success-ful than anywhere else in the world. Weak-kneed politi-cians are not altogether to blame, for obviously a smaller population (27 million in Canada) is easier to brainwash and manipulate than a larger one (250 million in the Unit-ed States, 56 million in the United Kingdom). In fact, histo-rians may well study feminism in Canada as a microcosm of the modern Women's Liberation Movement.

When the Canadian Charter of Rights and Freedoms on

April 17, 1985, *legislated* unbridled, unjustified discrimination against men in section 15, enshrining feminist ideology in the Canadian Constitution, telegrams poured across the border from all the feminist leaders in the United States, including Betty Friedan, congratulating feminist leaders in Canada in reaching their ultimate goal. (This achievement was comparable to the U.S. feminists' ultimate goal, the Equal Rights Amendment [ERA], which would have enshrined similar rights in the U.S. Constitution.)

Feminist writer Penny Kome in her book *The Taking of 28* boasted that Canadian feminists had given Canadians "the equivalent of ERA without anyone realizing it." She also points out that there were no more than 12 powerful feminist leaders who were responsible for this revolutionary accomplishment.

Human nature being what it is, there will always be some unjustified discrimination that human beings, men and women *together*, must address. There will always be blots on the pages of history. However, it now must be plain to see that this present blot can no longer be ignored. There is no justice that may be served by injustice.

Cunningly worded, the phrase in the Canadian Charter actually suggests that discrimination is permissible . . . if designed to help the disadvantaged. Immediately, the hundreds of federally and provincially funded women's councils and committees swung into action, mounting case after case before a Charter rights tribunal, which was swift to uphold the feminist theory: that men had been oppressing women and discriminating against them since time immemorial. Women were disadvantaged and therefore now "entitled" to retaliatory discrimination.

It was surprising that it took the majority of women across the country as long as it did to realize that it was indeed *their* husbands, *their* boyfriends, *their* fathers, *their* brothers, *their* sons who, sooner or later, would be directly affected. These women would come to see the threatened demise of *their* families, present and future, as husbands and fathers at every level of society were affected by such legislated programs as affirmative action, leapfrogging, and pay equity (equal pay for work of equal value). The decisions in pay equity are always arbitrary and seemingly made by "idiots," according to the multitude of complaints from businessmen who predict the demise of the small businesses particularly as a consequence of feminist rules.

It is sad that the effects of such programs are undoubtedly deterring many young men from seeking wives and looking forward to family lifestyles that would allow them a viable, principal role. It is even sadder that these young men may unjustly blame *all* women for the mountains of discrimination, faced in all areas, which can deprive them of a traditional, recognizable role.

As Nicholas Davidson in his book *The Failure of Feminism* and Stephen Heath in the anthology *Men in Feminism* have explained, men will simply *never* agree collectively to being poured into the contrived feminist mold. The psychologist Carl Jung, in *The Undiscovered Self,* had already warned us of the consequences when he discussed

the question of how the primordial images that maintain the flow of instinctive energy are to be reoriented or readapted. They cannot simply be replaced by a new rational configuration, for this would be molded too much by the outer situation and not enough by man's biological needs. Moreover, not only would it build no bridge to the original man, but it would block the approach to him altogether. This is in keeping with the aims of Marxist education, which seeks, like God himself, to mold man, but in the image of the State.[8]

Young men, conspicuously, have been deliberately

choosing to move into an all-male-centered world. Sigmund Freud in his *Civilization and Its Discontents* wrote: "Against the suffering which may come upon one from human relationships the readiest safeguard is voluntary isolation, keeping oneself aloof from other people."[9] Betty Friedan in *The Second Stage* wrote of all the young women who were worrying about the "culture of Narcissism" spreading throughout their male peer groups, with serious young men turning their backs on all women.[10]

My mother remarks: "When I see how feminists attempt to emasculate men, I am reminded of the old Bible story of Samson and Delilah. Delilah successfully destroyed Samson's powers when she cut off his hair, but Samson, with a last superhuman effort, reached for the pillars and pulled down the Temple on a whole race." It is a chilling thought, and I hasten to reassure her that such a conclusion could never be countenanced in the enlightened 1990s.

Men and women throughout the Western world, particularly younger men and women, are yearning for one another, are longing to overcome the separation of the sexes, are searching for the love and comfort and joy they may only find in being together again. They know that there have been only a few radical, powerful, militant Delilahs who have seduced a whole society, and that now they should be challenged. These men and women realize that the false premises in feminist ideology need to be questioned.

REVISIONISM

The continuing influence of "the few" cannot be minimized, and nowhere is it more insidious and far-reaching than in the feminist rewriting of history.

When the Centre for Women's Studies and Feminist Research opened with great fanfare at the University of Western Ontario in London, assistant professor Elizabeth Harvey explained: "What's happened is that, traditionally, in disciplines such as history, literature, philosophy, and so on, 'human being' or 'man' has been taken to mean 'male' or 'men.' The result has been a series of disciplines constructed around half of the human race." Allison Wylie, assistant professor of philosophy, discussing the status of women through the ages, discovered that any time there was a "renaissance," the flowering of a culture, "the position of women was substantially eroded. So, if you are going to look at women's experience and the status of women, you have to *restructure historical categories profoundly*" (my italics).

Professor Wylie has stated unequivocally that "all the existing disciplines are men's studies," and she and her colleagues now "adjust" history to illustrate how "various disciplines have been imbued with male-biased content and approaches."[11] Spurred on toward "justified" reverse discrimination, students learn that women must rewrite the history of the human race.

"In visual art, for example," Allison Wylie has stated, "the art forms which have tended to be the most celebrated in history, such as painting, have tended to be those associated with men." Yet women artists have been celebrated throughout the centuries, gaining international fame in their lifetimes and leaving as great a legacy as their male counterparts. Their works are hanging in all the great art galleries in the world, including the Louvre in Paris and the National Art Gallery in London.

Levine Teerlin became the most renowned miniaturist of her time, with her works as prominent at the courts of Henry VIII and Queen Elizabeth I as those of Hans Holbein. (Her works were also known to command higher prices.) Lady Elizabeth Butler, whose great battle scenes were among the most famous during Queen Victoria's reign, frequently exhibited her paintings in Buckingham Palace. In Marie Antoinette's France, Marie-Louise Elizabeth Vigee-LeBrun was a court portraitist. Although her magnificent portraits were to be saved, she herself, because of her close connection with the court, barely escaped the French Revolution with her life.[12]

In the realm of music, feminist writers dredge up a quarter of one percent of the women composers who believed they had to use men's names to get their works published — the American composers Carrie William Krogmann and Edith Borroff are popular examples, as is France's Augusta Mary Anne Holmes — ignoring the 6200 other renowned women composers who gained fame and fortune without subterfuge. Dame Ethel Smith was one of these. Indeed, women composers became famous and gained great prestige as far back as 2450 BC, when the Egyptian songstress Iti was honored throughout the Eastern world. In the eighth century AD, an Arabian songstress (whose name has been lost in antiquity) composed for and conducted the very first known touring orchestra — an ensemble of 50 Arabian women making the pilgrimage from Medina to Mecca.[13]

When lesbian writers attempt to draw such beloved authors as Willa Cather into their orbit by suggesting she was lesbian; and other feminist writers insinuate that the poetic works of the Wordsworths should be mainly attributed to Dorothy rather than her brother, William; and claim that authors of such classic stature as Jane Austen and the Brontës are not properly revered in our culture; and that male writers have never elevated heroines to the same heights as heroes — then, I believe, academia itself has become peopled with Golda Meier's "crazies." Surely it must be time to demand a halt to the feminists' attempts to rewrite history into *her*story.

Denis Donoghue in *Men in Feminism*, discussing "all prior literary histories . . . rendered partial, inadequate, and obsolete" by feminist writers, wonders "whether these sentiments, which seem wild to me, accurately indicate the context of feminist criticism or some bizarre hyperbole; a real fury in the words, or willed turbulence worked up for the occasion." Furthermore, he explains, books such as the new *Norton Anthology of Literature by Women* are simply "assembled documentary evidence to support a case against men," and are "flagrantly misleading as a selection of literature by women."[14]

John Ruskin was illustrating Shakespeare's veneration of women in his *Sesame and Lillies* lecture, published in 1907:

> In his laboured and perfect plays you have no hero
> . . . only heroines. Othello would have been one, if
> his simplicity had not been so great as to leave him
> the prey of every base practice round him; Coriolanus
> — Caesar — Antony, stand in flawed strength, and
> fall by their vanities; Hamlet is indolent, Romeo an
> impatient boy; the Merchant of Venice languidly sub-
> missive to adverse fortune; Kent, in King Lear, is en-
> tirely noble at heart, but too rough and unpolished to
> be of true use at the critical time . . . Orlando, no
> less noble, is yet the despairing toy of chance . . .
> saved by Rosalind.
>   Whereas there is hardly a play that has not a per-
> fect woman in it, steadfast in grave hope and error-
> less purpose: Cordelia, Desdemona, Isabella,
> Hermione, Imogen, Queen Katherine, Perdita, Sylvia,
> Viola, Rosalind, Helena, and last, and perhaps loveli-
> est, Virgilia . . . all are faultless; conceived in the high-
> est heroic type of humanity.[15]

But one would be hard-pressed to find any of John Ruskin's works on the library shelves in the women's stud-ies department of any university across the North American continent.

George Gilder, author of the bestseller *Sexual Terrorism*,

claims that every year "25,000 innocent co-eds have been transformed into dedicated ruthless libbers" in the women's studies courses in North American universities. "These courses constitute the most brutal brainwashing since Josef Stalin introduced compulsory nursery school in the Soviet Union."[16]

Professor Ruth R. Wisse writes:

> The Bolshevik tactics introduced by the women's movement have permeated university life, and each time they are resorted to afresh, verbally if not physically, the university reacts as I once did: it acquiesces in the "foolishness" as a kind of temporary, temporizing measure, assuming that it will make no difference, even as it goes on making all the difference in the world.
>
> The Bolsheviks did not storm the palace . . . they did not have to. The idea of woman-as-victim seeped into the culture the way environmentalists tell us chemical wastes leach into our water and soil. Relations between men and women, upon which more than upon any other clause of the social contract, the species depends, were redefined, in terms of "power." Young couples took to arguing like trade unionists over whose turn it was to change the baby's diaper.[17]

The message was clear: that young husband must now do twice his "share" because his great-great-grandfather had discriminated against women. Great-great-grandfather never realized he should have been changing diapers, making butter and the breakfast porridge, as well as milking his 10 cows, felling the trees and setting the wolf traps. Many modern men still can't visualize being pitcher and catcher on the same baseball team.

The young woman who does not wish to deny her des

ignated vocation of nurturing the young within her womb and at her breast may also look back to that great-great-grandfather. He may help her to understand that the majority of nonfeminist men today still believe they should fill *one* position on the team — milking the cows, felling the trees, keeping the wolf from the door — or at least be principally responsible for that *one* position on the team.

4
Rampant, Unjustified Reverse Discrimination

Mary Wollstonecraft is credited with writing the first great feminist protest against men's so-called dominance in society. Her book *The Vindication of Women*, published in 1792 and today having assumed biblical proportions in women's studies, certainly gave birth to the myth that men were always deliberately and unjustifiably discriminating against women.

Her hatred of men obviously knew no bounds, and her targets included her father, whose misfortunes in business she treated with the utmost contempt; her lover, the American Gilbert Imlay with whom she lived in Paris during the French Revolution, who deserted her following the birth of their daughter, Fanny; and her brother-in-law, from whom she would attempt to rescue her sister, Eliza (although later Eliza complained bitterly of Mary's interference, which had threatened Eliza's marriage). Her greatest rage and resentment, however, seems to have been directed against her brother, Ned. Not only was he their mother's favorite, but, as a "privileged male," he would inherit money that enabled him to train to become a successful lawyer, a profession that Mary herself may have coveted.

Of course, in her era it was unthinkable that limited family funds could be given to daughters for education rather than to male heirs. Daughters would normally marry and bear children and run households, and indeed they were known to have few other aspirations. What is particularly ironic is that the author herself eventually found the traditional female lifestyle idyllic when she married her publisher, William Godwin. Before she died in 1797 (giving birth to another Mary, who also became a famous author and was a most loving wife of the English poet Percy Bysshe Shelley), she was extolling marriage as "the foundation of almost every social virtue," potentially a "microcosm of social harmony."[1]

Still, modern feminism would glorify Mary as the perfect example of a woman of the past who suffered discrimination in a so-called patriarchy, and it would condemn brother Ned, the "privileged male" who had fallen heir to the family fortune and the education that permitted him to achieve a law degree. Quite simply, this was the basis of the premise which demands that all modern females now be allowed to even the score.

Evening the score in all areas of postsecondary school education, with rampant, unjustified reverse discrimination, has been under way in the past decades, remaining unchecked today under feminist dictatorship. In Canada, where the feminist dictatorship flexes its power almost on a daily basis throughout the educational system, cases such as the appointment of a new dean of Toronto's Osgoode Hall Law School (at York University) are not atypical.

When York University President Harry Arthurs chose an outsider, James Currie MacPherson, over an associate dean, Mary Jane Mossman, feminists filed an immediate charge of discrimination with the Ontario Human Rights Commission, promising dire penalties. Because the York University

Staff Association was already 85 percent female, President Arthurs may have expected the torrents of vilification that would rain down on him during the hearings, duly repeated in all media from coast to coast. This publicity would naturally further intimidate any other educational heads who dared to step over feminist guidelines. In vain, President Arthurs argued:

> The Osgoode deanship race was chosen as a high-profile occasion for feminist lawyers to make some points they have been wanting to make for a long time . . . directed as they are to us . . . these charges are groundless; they are irresponsible.
>
> The female applicant possesses only "acceptable" skills as a legal scholar and lacked a willingness to tackle personally the problems of the law school, while the male applicant was perceived to have greater abilities and willingness to move the law school forward . . .
>
> [Furthermore] it was important to have a dean from outside the school as schools tend to become somewhat introspective and relationships tend to solidify as people work together over a long period of time.[2]

His record of already appointing two female deans out of nine at the university, and his reputation for instructing search committees to look for qualified women candidates, proved inconsequential. Although the appointment could not be canceled, heavy penalties included the university's spending another million dollars on women's studies as well as its setting up a substantial scholarship in the failed applicant's name — penalties the university could ill afford in a time of government cutbacks.

When will society begin to realize that the quality of higher education is already suffering as a result of an unbalanced quota system that sees undergraduate programs weeding out promising male candidates? When will it question a policy that sees feminists unjustifiably enforcing the dredging up and appointment of less qualified candidates merely because they are women?

In January 1990, the Board of Governors of the Ontario College of Art, Canada's premier art school, announced it would not accept *any* male applications for its professorial positions during the next *10 years*, even while admitting that the number of female applicants in past years had been minimal. That same month, Ryerson Polytechnical Institute in Toronto, Canada's leading English-speaking technical college, refused to accept *any* male teacher's application for one department, and for another department it eliminated teaching positions held by males under contract to make way for women to proceed toward tenure.

Ryerson vice president Larry Gray sympathized with the dismissed male professors, explaining that this was "legislated discrimination."[3]

There is no doubt that women do have to be dredged up through the ranks while highly qualified male applicants are arbitrarily turned down in every discipline. However, feminist leaders believe that blocking male candidates from traditionally male-dominated teaching positions at the undergraduate level will eventually result in feminist domination of all disciplines.

By 1982, 59.2 percent of all master's degrees in the health professions in Canada were granted to women, according to Statistics Canada. By 1986, female enrolment in pharmacy studies was 69.9 percent of the total, and by 1990 the number of drugstores owned or managed by women had increased significantly. It is estimated that more than 63 percent of medical students across North America are women, and a 1988 study by the Association of Canadian Medical Colleges showed a 25 percent drop in male applications since 1973. This decrease is explained by some students as the result of an unwillingness to face unfair competition, such as that practiced at McMaster University in Hamilton, Ontario, where 61 percent of the first-year spaces are automatically offered to women.[4]

Does all this signify a lethargy of defeat among our young men, generally — the very individuals from whom we might expect leadership in restoring reason and balance, in overcoming feminist-dictated legislation that is so decisively separating the sexes? Perhaps they have simply been waiting for the understanding of the young women who will join their ranks. The majority of the population is already "onside." A 1989 University of Toronto study indicated that in surveys of Canadians generally and of 1125 federal and provincial justice department politicians, 66 percent in each group condemns quota systems.[5]

A dean of ophthalmology of the University of Toronto told me that a few years ago the faculty had decided to train 10 women ophthalmologists; within 10 years of graduation, however, only one was practicing. "We didn't realize we were discriminating against women when we continued to admit more men than women into the program," he explained. "We believed that we were simply acting reasonably to provide the necessary numbers of ophthalmologists in the province."

Although greater dedication is demanded of female medical specialists today, the serious repercussions of reverse discrimination are now being experienced across the continent, threatening all areas in medical care. Statistics record that the majority of female medical graduates shy away from time-consuming specialties, usually opting for family practice. By the late 1980s, extreme shortages in specialties such as ophthalmology, anesthesiology, surgery, radiology and orthopedics, fields in which a man's superior strength is often required, had become alarming. Of even greater concern is the fact that few women doctors can be persuaded to leave the larger cities to practice in smaller centers of remote areas. A 1989 Canadian Medical

Association survey of 38,600 members found that women doctors practicing full-time work fewer hours than men and retire earlier, while significant numbers of women doctors are not practicing at all.[6]

Still, particularly in Canada, feminists continue to drive women past men into all science courses, using discriminatory incentives that include government-funded female-only scholarships. In 1990, as part of a pilot project for schools across the country to follow, the Ottawa Board of Education instituted a girls-only mathematics program in 10 of its grade 6 classes — denying grade 6 boys access to such specialized education.[7]

How could such blatant injustices be sanctioned throughout our educational systems? This, apparently, was not a topic up for discussion at a women-in-science symposium at York University at which Professor Jim Megaw admitted that 90 percent of girls choose to drop out of physics in high school in Canada, a number that remains constant in the United Kingdom as well as in Australia.[8]

The *New York Times* reported that a third of the women who received Master of Business Administration degrees in 1976 had, by 1986, left management ranks, the majority to raise children.[9] More recently, financial magazines have considered the repercussions stemming from the exclusion of many able male students from such programs to make way for the female influx under the quota systems. The results could have an adverse effect on American industry and commerce generally, owing to loss of competence and uninterrupted dedication to a job.

Although it is estimated that the number of female law students now outnumber male law students across the continent, surveys suggest that many women lawyers have become disenchanted with the profession and are leaving it in ever-increasing numbers. A report by the Canadian Bar Association states that "women lawyers are more likely than men to choose non-traditional careers . . . for reasons related to childbirth and child care." Many women have also found that "they are uncomfortable with the adversarial and competitive nature of the job. Studies show that women are "conciliatory rather than competitive," one woman lawyer was quoted as saying.[10]

It's a "workaholic profession," extremely hard to combine with any family or social commitments, particularly if involved with litigation, Toronto lawyer Judith Wolfson explained. "At the senior level it is almost impossible to reduce the hours, as witnesses must be interviewed and cases prepared after court."[11]

Nevertheless, statistics prove that female lawyers manage to work more than 30 percent fewer hours than male lawyers, while often avoiding travel and night meetings. Legal firms calculate an employee's worth on billable hours, and so there is little wonder that few women lawyers reach partner status, with the corresponding salary. Yet feminists continue to scream "discrimination."

Internationally respected poetess Joy Kogawa, the author of the award-winning novel *Obasan*, warned us:

> There comes a point when screaming victimization begins to victimize others . . . I think it's time someone did a thorough criticism of what now passes for feminism . . . There comes a point in any movement where what was healthy and wholesome turns into something quite pernicious and death-producing . . .
>
> We've lost the sacral view of life because of our mendacity . . . I feel so overwhelmed by the lying in our society . . .[12]

In bringing men and women together again, surely it is time that we all begin to face the truth: to understand that men, usually, were not deliberately discriminating against women throughout the ages. Historically, men had simply adopted the role of so-called patriarch as social conditions of the times dictated. Yes; men certainly saw themselves as protectors of womankind — the nurturers of offspring in the continuance of the human species.

Surely it is time we all understand that modern men do not deserve the cruel and unjust punishment of rampant reverse discrimination, meted out in programs such as affirmative action, as a penalty for those so-called sins of their forefathers.

Honesty is the crucible. Justice cannot be served by injustice.

5

The Ugly Face of Androgyny

Feminism like socialism can succeed only through its control of an amorphous mass, the concept explained in Lenin's writings. Soon it seemed clear to feminist leaders in the Western world that men and women throughout society, and particularly in the workplace, must be leveled into such a mass. It was time to introduce another false premise into the Women's Liberation Movement, in the theory of Androgyny.

Androgyny, an unlikely word in anyone's vocabulary except that of a biologist, was soon rolling off everyone's tongue, becoming as popular as the feminist expression "consciousness-raising." Women in their consciousness-raising groups were then indoctrinated into believing that baby girls and baby boys came into this world absolutely equal in strengths — psychological and biological — like little jellyfish on the shore that could be molded, this way or that way. Anything else was called stereotyping, and it became a mortal sin henceforth to engage in sexist stereotyping, such as giving dolls to the little girls and trucks and hammers to the little boys.

Historians surely will eventually marvel at the impact of this new feminist con game. Mona Charen in an article in the *National Review* wrote: "Perhaps my grandchildren will look back on our era as socially aberrant — 'Did they really want boys and girls to be the same, Grandma?'"[1] I heard Jane Pauley, the television anchor, who is the mother of twins, ask feminist, and childless, Marlo Thomas on the *Today Show*, "Have you really ever watched how little girls and little boys play and noticed how they naturally gravitate toward those supposedly 'stereotyping' toys?"

The august *Roget's Thesaurus* gives the following synonyms for androgynous: mongrel, hybrid, epicene, denaturalized. Certainly the denaturalization of men and women had begun, and within a very few years — inconceivably — it was legislated throughout our culture.

It was Margaret Mead, with her pseudoscientific conclusions to her studies of primitive cultures, who would lead North American women directly down another garden path. As a young anthropologist, she had gone to Samoa in 1925 and New Guinea in 1931. Whether she was merely very young, or just inexperienced, or had simply envisaged the results of her observations — results on which she hoped to base a new and noteworthy view of human society — we will never know. We do know that she came back with some astonishing findings which would bring her almost instant fame.

The denaturalization of men and women was born in her contrived theory of androgyny: all biological and psychic forces in human nature, in men and women, were indistinguishable; our lifestyles throughout the ages had simply been the consequence of "cultural patterning."

An accomplished writer whose books would quickly appear on the bestseller lists, Margaret Mead was heralded as the authoritative feminist guru of the Women's Liberation Movement — offering women "liberation" from all moral restraints and a true egalitarian society in which men and women could be absolutely equal in every area — all biological and psychic considerations to be ignored. Readers would be persuaded, often simply by her use of scientific language, sometimes obtuse to the most educated, of all the advantages in achieving equality in such liberation. In her book *Coming of Age in Samoa*, Margaret Mead described an idyllic paradise where the aspirations and roles of boys and girls were interchangeable, and where parental permissiveness allowed unleashed promiscuity (reflected in our youth today). It all sounded so delightful, and natural, and right. In her book *Sex and Temperament in Three Primitive Societies*, she wrote:

> The personality traits which we have called masculine and feminine are as lightly linked to sex as are the clothing, the manners, and the form of head-dress that a society at a given period assigns to either sex . . . the differences between individuals who are members of different cultures, like the difference between individuals within a culture, are almost entirely to be laid to differences in conditioning, especially during early childhood. Standardized personality differences between the sexes are of this order, cultural creations to which each generation, male and female, is trained to conform.[2]

In the multitude of books and articles that flowed from other feminist writers who enforced this message, the goal of ultimate equality between the sexes was established. Such a goal could be attained — ensuring that amorphous mass — by denying a man's superior prowess and by ignoring a woman's biological concerns. Why, Margaret Mead even led us to believe that an egalitarian society produced "feminized" personality traits in both men and women. Dissenting voices would be silenced in the controlled feminist press.

The flaws, the obvious contradictions and the outright lies in Margaret Mead's studies were finally exposed by a well-respected Australian anthropologist, Derek Freeman, in his 1983 book *Margaret Mead and Samoa*.[3] A barrage of feminist vilification attempted to drown out the truth, but the books and scientific papers that followed offered corroborating evidence.

Margaret Mead offered no defense, even suggesting that she herself had always considered her research "plastic." It is ironic that before she died she seemed to be questioning the very results of androgyny and feminist ideology generally. She wrote:

> Families are in trouble everywhere in a world in which change . . . kinds of change that in many cases we ourselves proudly initiated . . . has been massive and rapid, and innovations have proliferated with only the most superficial concern for their effect on human lives . . .
>
> At a turning point . . . it becomes crucial to redefine what we most value and where we are headed.[4]

Scientists worldwide have made us understand that Margaret Mead's theory of androgyny is an utterly false premise, yet we continue to live under a system, based on lies, that enforces equality of the sexes. Nicholas Davidson, in his book *The Failure of Feminism*, explains:

> The hoary untruths of Mead's 1931 research are taught to successive generations of students . . . At every major college and university, students are trained to revere cultural determinism as a pillar of freedom and to despise behavioral biology as a naive superstition . . . Mead's obsolete views on sex and temperament have been virtually written into the U.S.

Constitution . . .

To continue to ignore the relevance of the biological to human affairs . . . is no longer possible, unless we are to despair completely of the quest for truth and define science as merely a branch of ideology.[5]

Indeed, how can we be successful in bringing men and women together again if we do not understand that we must bring truth and justice back into our culture, back into our lives? How can we succeed if we do not do something about laws that are not based on truth and justice? We must revoke those laws that are blatantly discriminatory and adjust others to minimize the devastating long-term effects on families. Of course, these efforts will have little hope of success without equal participation by men and women . . . together again.

Society generally, I believe, began to recognize the ugliness of androgyny by the late 1970s, seeing the feminist premise based on it as nothing less than a doctrine dictating the denaturalization of men and women. By the early 1980s it was obvious that men were resisting such dictatorship, and the groundswell gradually, if silently, accelerated throughout that decade.

After spending a day in the mines, or 14 hours driving and unloading a truck, or 12 harried hours in an executive boardroom, or 15 hours in a congressional committee meeting, men were simply refusing to knuckle down under a dictatorship that ordered them out of the workplace of their choice and into the kitchens and the nurseries of the land. (In the nurseries many of them showed a wretched lack of aptitude — they simply did not have the baby's milk in their bosoms. At the same time, all those indoctrinated women happily put on the man's suit and strutted down Wall Street, or climbed the fireman's ladder, or joined the army — their bosoms round and full and carrying the baby's milk.)

The Ontario Government spent $20,000 on a poster campaign to attract elementary school girls to careers in police work and firefighting. Spending billions of taxpayers' dollars, Canada leads all countries with its programs training women for all traditionally male fields, such as welding, mining and forestry. The provinces by law must guarantee a 30 percent female representation in all trades, although this quota proves impossible; in welding, for instance, female applicants are often as scarce as hen's teeth. By law, female apprentices receive a 25 percent subsidy, while government funds traditionally available for apprenticeship programs for young males are no longer forthcoming.

Statistics Canada reported that 94 percent of all newly created jobs were taken by women between 1981 and 1986. The United States Bureau of Labor Statistics in 1983 listed women as comprising 43 percent of the overall labor force and estimated that the figure would increase to over 60 percent by the 1990s.[6] All future estimates will of course be quite changed as government statisticians take into account the new exodus from the workplace of rethinking young women who no longer will deny their yearning to care for their precious babies.

Even older women who once believed their feet were cemented into feminist culture are answering to the needs of their teenagers and returning home. One such mother, speaking on a Canadian Broadcasting Corporation *Sunday Morning* radio program that looked at the demise of the family (December 9, 1990), described her return home to her teenagers. She claimed she was meeting the greatest challenges of her life, far greater than any she had ever encountered.

In studying the Canadian experience as a microcosm of the modern feminist movement throughout the Western world, it is certainly of the greatest importance to note the key role feminist leaders throughout the labor unions have played in the achievement of feminist goals. The proportion of female members in labor organizations has been twice as high in Canada as in the United States, and their dominating influence is recognized in their preoccupation with all feminist goals, with success after success crowning their efforts. They take full credit for such legislation as pay equity, extended maternity leave with pay, pension benefits for transient part-time workers, and female training programs. And they are moving closer and closer to achieving their ultimate goal of state-funded Universal Day Care; children as young as four already are being legislated into many educational systems.

Shirley Carr, the dynamic president of the Canadian Labour Congress (and a former New Democrat provincial candidate), and executive vice president Nancy Riche, another powerful feminist leader, have represented 2.1 million members in 78 affiliated unions — 58 percent of all unionized members in Canada. With the influence of other feminist leaders throughout the upper echelons of all unions added on, it is estimated that union membership in Canada will soon resemble that of socialist Sweden, where women make up 91 percent of new union members.[7]

There is absolutely no doubt that male union members have become increasingly resentful of the affirmative action programs, quota systems and pay equity laws under which they now believe they have become extremely disadvantaged. Yet they still seem as intimidated as the majority of politicians throughout the Western world, who are afraid to speak out. Are they really offering such little resistance within the ranks? Off the record, they are extremely vocal.

Initially, male union members certainly welcomed women into their ranks. The women were an asset on the picket lines, often dragging their little children around and around with them, a sight that would bring their causes instant public support. Because they were able to rely on a husband's second salary in the majority of cases, women could stay out on the line much longer than could a sole-supporting husband and father, thus prolonging the strike. And they would tighten up all union policies and demands, insisting on a strict adherence to contracts — actually a rigidity that would affect all commerce. This rigidity, from the point of view of the business world, was truly revolutionary: women at two minutes past five o'clock were out of the offices and factories on their way to pick up the kids from day care; male workers, formerly easygoing and willing to remain unpaid for finishing a job, would henceforth be paid, probably double, for every split second of their extra time.

In those earlier years, male union members even failed to complain when their customary weekend union meetings were so often switched to weeknights, as an accommodation to women who refused to leave their families on weekends. Eventually, some male union members complained that they were too tired to participate in those meetings, which, invariably, turned into political strategy sessions and often concentrated on nothing other than feminist issues such as the drive toward Universal Day Care.

Male union members generally will admit that they applauded the government and company subsidies for day care, an early and major accomplishment of powerful feminist trade unionists. They realized that this was the encouragement their wives needed to go out and get jobs that would bring in a second salary. However, too often the result was two exhausted parents and an uncomfortable, an unhappy and, subsequently, a broken home.

Their feminist leaders' crowning achievement of pay equity laws and the establishment of the enforcement bureaucracies would be recognized, however, as female dominance. Male workers at every stratum would be ghettoized: trapped at one level and denied advancement and raises, while women of supposedly "comparable worth" rose above them to drain the company coffers.

But the anger mounted when, suddenly, middle-aged workers began to see their sons denied the apprenticeships and jobs that were given to women who often had to be cajoled into even applying for them. I was told of the unbearable distress of one man whose son, who had always expected to follow in his father's trade, was turned down for three jobs for which he was fully qualified, became despondent and developed into a drifter. One of the three women accepted in place of that son was on maternity leave within the year.

Because unions are an integral part of our democracies, and have generally been led by reasonable, dedicated and often great individuals — Lech Walesa, for example — I believe fathers and mothers in union ranks will soon provide the leadership in restoring reason and balance to the workplace. Their efforts to defeat the injustices of affirmative action, leapfrogging, quota systems and pay equity will surely go a long way toward reconciling the differences between the sexes.

First of all, the feminist theory of androgyny, the equality of the sexes, will have to be debunked, exposed as the deceit it is. Given the urgency of the task, the job will prove of the greatest magnitude. The propaganda launched to spread the theory throughout society no doubt was as carefully planned as were the shuttles launched into outer space.

The cajoling of women and society generally into believing that the sexes can be denaturalized has been witnessed in an unparalleled propaganda campaign which tells us that women particularly can ignore biology and all emotional aspirations and aptitudes and instincts; that they are absolutely equal to men in all aspects and therefore must be legislated in equal numbers into all former traditionally male occupations (although men are not legislated in equal numbers into all former traditionally female occupations). Feminist leaders who control the print media, and who still seem capable of silencing all dissenting opinions, have fed us a never-ending stream of news items and articles featuring remarkable women with the prowess to handle any job as well as any man.

Forty-five-year-old Sergeant Cheryl Ingwerson, head of the Metro Toronto Police Cadet Program, "doesn't act tough," marveled a newspaper reporter in a major front-page feature article that appeared in newspapers across Canada, "but she says she can fight like a tiger — proving she's not timid about potentially violent situations. She has been beaten up twice, ironically both times by a woman." In her own words she described an incident when a woman being searched "went absolutely berserk. It took three guys to hold her down. She nearly took my face off. She tried to take my eyes out."

Sergeant Ingwerson also recalled trying to apprehend a man in a park for allegedly molesting young girls. He knocked her down but she grabbed on to his arm and refused to let go. "I got dragged across Allan Gardens. I had him under arrest but he wasn't stopping," she said, adding that other police officers finally arrived to assist her.[8]

"Feminizing" the forces must be accomplished according to Canadian law, and the Metro Toronto Police Force has become a leader in such an effort: 51 percent of its civilian staff and 33 percent of its 1990 class of prospective police officers are women, and there is an aggressive recruitment program for women.

Hundreds of thrilling stories lauding remarkable women performing in nontraditional jobs as well as or better than a man are repeated over and over. Dianne Oland, a Toronto firefighter, became a celebrity thanks to a number of feature articles appearing in all national newspapers. Half-page photographs showed her wearing "a triple-lined coat, hip-wader boots, carrying a 50-pound breathing apparatus on her back, and working from a truck with a ladder that extended ten stories high"; and she would boast, happily, that "you'll be lucky if you get three hours' sleep on your 14-hour night shift."[9]

Billie Padilla, a divorced mother of two, became famous as the first female longshorewoman — a stevedore — on the Pacific west coast. Major articles illustrated her competence at the Los Angeles-Long Beach port, where she moved "50-pound banana boxes" and lashed "cargo containers together 200 feet up in the air."[10] A story to match was that of Dean Pizzy, a 35-year-old wife and mother, fighting forest fires 118 miles west of Winnipeg. She was shown carrying a heavy water pump on her back and pulling hundreds of meters of soggy hose through dense bush after setting up camp.[11]

An Ontario construction company given a $400,000 grant by the federal government to train women roadbuilders reported that there were a few women who had survived the course. "They were the muscular types who aren't bothered by slugging through ten-hour days in the sweltering sun, hauling bags of cement and wallowing in hot, sticky, smelly asphalt," an official explained.[12]

The wages often commanded by extremely dangerous work for a woman are always a factor in luring women to such jobs. Cat Duly, an operator of a front-end loader in the construction of the SkyDome in Toronto, became an admirable example of equality in the workplace, earning $60,000 a year.[13]

When a small construction company refused to hire a woman for a similar job, it faced a costly court battle in which $30,000 was awarded the complainant. The manager had pleaded that he truly believed no woman was strong enough to handle the equipment (and I myself heard the complainant on the radio confessing that she "had trouble with the fork-lift trucks"). In another of hundreds of such cases in Canada, Elaine McAra was awarded

$31,135 for suffering "mental anguish" as a result of being refused warehouse work that involved extremely heavy lifting. One must wonder if these stiff penalties are designed to put small companies out of business, if they are unwarranted punishment for so-called discrimination against women.[14]

Large companies able to afford a fortune for their defense fare no better in the courts. When Canadian National Railways was forced to accept women as yard workers, the president of the company said he could "guarantee" that some of those women would simply be "standing in a corner," absolutely incapable of handling the weights. When Stelco, Canada's largest manufacturer, was forced to put one lone woman in its boiler division in Hamilton, Ontario, the worker went to court to demand an adjacent washroom. The company not only paid $20,000 to install the washroom for that lone female worker, but was also ordered to pay her $5000 as compensation for the "harassment" she claimed she was subjected to in graffiti that obviously expressed male resentment of her forced intrusion into a more comfortable, all-male bastion.[15]

There are fearsome elements, in my opinion, in the Canadian KGB — the feminist watchdogs in LEAF (Legal Education and Action Fund), which is funded by the federal government. Many believe that they deliberately seek out prospective victims of so-called discrimination to bring before cooperating human rights tribunals and "feminized" courts.

Eddie Greenspan, prominent Canadian criminal lawyer and the author of *Greenspan*, in which he covers the injustices now perpetrated in Canadian courts, has stated flatly that "the law itself has become feminized."[16]

PERFORMANCE

The ignoring of biology in feminist ideology, in the denaturalization of women, has been a bizarre attempt to deny the proven absolutes in the findings of the greatest ancient and modern-day scientists. We know that the word biology comes from the Greek *bios*, meaning life, and *logos*, meaning study. This science was considered the basis of all learning by Aristotle, Hippocrates (the first physician), Dioscorides and Pliny, the Roman general who gave us 37 volumes of natural history recording the life and biological capabilities of plants and primates. Today, hundreds of scholars explain how men and women are different from each other — unequal — biologically and psychologically. Men are far superior to women in some areas, and women far more capable than men in other areas.

Gender Identity, an anthology edited by Nicholas Davidson, meticulously documents such modern-day findings. Contributor Michael Levin, a Rutgers University philosopher, warns of the extreme peril, mental and physical, in the indoctrination of the children of North America that is under way in all educational programs. In establishing androgyny, it distorts reality, neuters the sexes and reverses roles. His extensive studies of the differences in the brain formations, in the hormones and in the behavioral patterns of men and women are reported in his book, *Feminism and Freedom*. There is ample evidence that feminists have attempted to suppress both these books.[17]

There are fish that fly and there are birds that swim, and there are marvelous women who are equal to men in physical and psychological strength, capable of performing any job as well as any man. However, enforcing the feminist theory of androgyny in legislation — affirmative action, leapfrogging, pay equity (the Canadian term) and comparative worth (the U.S. term) — on the basis of the performance of a very few such women is a gross aberration in societal judgment and justice. Such policies must be reconsidered if men and women are to be brought together again.

Michael Levin consistently points out that laws enforcing

androgyny are simply "the feminist road to socialism,"[18] and economists gloomily forecast the results: the steady erosion of North American capitalism and the smothering of entrepreneurial ambition in many young men.

Janet Radcliffe Richards in her book *The Skeptical Feminist* asks:

> What about employers who are made to employ women who will do the work less well than men would have done, like the ones at present who are not allowed to take public suspicion of women into consideration? . . . This is the sort of thing Robert Nozick, in his book, *Anarchy, State and Utopia*, would count as forced labour.[19]

Sociologist Brigitte Berger of Wellesley College writes:

> Both career pattern differences [between men and women], as well as income differences, can be explained — and to my mind convincingly — in terms of women's . . . overall life plans.[20]

As early as 1984, Barbara Amiel, *Maclean's* magazine columnist and a former editor of the *Toronto Sun*, was explaining that the Women's Liberation Movement in Canada

> has managed to get a stranglehold on our policymakers . . . and in opening the doors of state interference and in the denial of reality in order to fit everything into its members' warped ideological mold, it will wreak havoc with the lives of us all — men, women and children.[21]

Think tanks across the continent, among them the Fraser Institute in Vancouver, have since the 1970s published hundreds of statistics proving that single women without dependants, with the same dedication and drive as single men without dependants, have received equal or in many instances considerably higher pay than those men. Yet the statistics also suggest that overall performance of females in the workplace in no way can be compared with that of males, a fact that justifies traditional differences in pay scales.

Conflict between work and families accounts for women being responsible for 25 percent of all employee absenteeism, according to a 1988 Conference Board of Canada survey of 385 companies. (The companies could not be identified because of a guarantee of confidentiality.)[22]

A *Harvard Business Review* article, based on two major studies, proved that the turnover rate of women in multinational corporations is two and a half times higher than that of men.[23] The Corning Glass Company in New York State claimed that its records showed women were twice as likely as men to leave the company, and that the cost of replacing female employees was two million dollars a year. A consumers' goods organization reported that of the women in its industry taking maternity leave, 50 percent either came back late or not at all.[24] And the United States Department of Labor published the findings of a major study estimating that "the number of years men stay on their jobs exceeds that for women by 77 to 100 percent."

"Men usually show a dedication, with a long-time view of their jobs totally different from that of many women in the workforce," one company executive was quoted as saying. "I think women, fed on feminism, have this high and mighty attitude that it is *their right* to take or leave a job, to change jobs, to take time off, or to reduce their hours, without any penalties whatever. I've met few women, married, mothers, or singles, who will put in the extra hours that are absolutely vital at peak points or in certain emergency situations — those extra hours that a man, unionized or not, expects and usually willingly accepts as part of his overall contribution to a company's viability in a competitive market."[25]

The Canadian Manufacturers' Association compiled statistics showing that women on the job work 30 percent fewer hours than men. Under feminist laws, employers must compensate women for absenteeism due not only to family concerns and pregnancies but also to projected premenstrual syndrome (PMS) and menopausal problems.

The American Medical Association designates PMS a disease, "affecting up to 40 percent of all women between the ages of 30 to 40, lasting between four to 14 days, with mental and physical symptoms ranging from suicidal depression, with weeping and forgetfulness, to extreme abdominal pain and general physical malaise." (Even that fun television series *Murphy Brown* acknowledges the influence of PMS, with Frank noting that "all the guys in the office have the 18th of the month marked on their calendar, the time to keep out of Murph's way."[26]

A McGill University study, reported in *Canadian Living*, found that 50 percent of all women have significant difficulties with the menopause, with another 25 percent requiring medical help to manage all the physical and mental problems involved (only two of which are the hot flashes and confusion). Former Chicago mayor, Jane M. Byrne, was nicknamed "Hot-Flash Jane" and accused of being "menopausally unhinged" when she came under the scrutiny of a state grand jury for allegedly mishandling state funds.[27]

While feminist propaganda lauds the large corporations able to establish day care facilities on their premises, where mothers can tend to their work and their children — sometimes simultaneously — smaller business operations are unable to contemplate such expenditures.

Some smaller companies do make incredible efforts, such as the Rempel Trail Transportation Company of northern British Columbia, which has proposed a 14-hour, seven-day-a-week day care program for the children of female truckers on the long hauls. Still, Gordon Boal, president of the Alberta Trucking Association, admits regretfully that it is almost impossible to fill the required female quota of truckers: few women are able to handle the 55 kilograms (120 pounds) of chains that must be hooked on to a rig in the winter and not many are willing to spend weeks away from their families.[28]

The number of women who leave jobs at which, they finally realize, they are totally unfit for — physically or psychologically — are legion. In 1986, the Toronto branch of the United Brotherhood of Carpenters and Joiners was forced to take on 20 women as apprentices. In 1987, only seven remained in the trades — causing a serious shortage in a booming building cycle. Meanwhile, 13 qualified young men had been denied those apprenticeships and the resulting jobs — perhaps their life work.[29]

Charlie Brown, program chief, explained: "Women find the physical aspect of the jobs very heavy . . . and the shift work and early hours very difficult for their families." (I was told by another official that some of those seven remaining women have also left.)

Prominent Toronto lawyer Maureen Sabia is quoted as saying: "Affirmative action programs are disastrous . . . Their very existence proves the point that women are unable to compete with men on any equal footing. The feminists, instead of teaching women to 'adapt' to the workplace, have simply been determined to dismantle and transform the workplace to suit their own, and sometimes transient aspirations."[30]

In the United States, Democrat Representative Pat Shroeder has been continually thwarted in floating her bills through the House that would put women in the front lines of battle. Yet in 1990 the ultimate success of the theory of androgyny — the equality of the sexes — was recognized in the presence of American women in all army, navy and air force detachments in the Persian Gulf. However, "this is where the feminists may have come a cropper," according to a Tennessee captain, a former horseman-reservist who served in Operation Desert Storm.

Genevieve Henderson, a member of a media pool covering Fort Carson troop activity in Saudi Arabia, in a front-page article in the *Colorado Springs Gazette Telegraph,* reported that women were "rethinking duty on front lines." The women she interviewed were thoroughly disenchanted with all the frontier conditions, including lack of privacy and sanitation, as well as with the buildup of sexual tensions.

"I don't think women should be over here. They can't handle it," Sergeant Wendy Thornton told her. Sergeant Thornton had joined the army five years before, right out of high school. Among the first women ordered to the Persian Gulf, she was driving a five-ton tractor-trailer hauling water across the desert. "Those feminists back home who say we have a right to fight are not out here sitting in the heat, carrying an M-16 and a gas mask, spending 16 hours on the road every day and sleeping in fear you're gonna get gassed."

Private April Rolle of the 360th "could not control her anguish and began sobbing when asked about her two children," the article reported. "It's like this: I'm a woman before I'm a soldier . . . Out here I think more about my family than my job, and yes, that could affect my performance if things got intense here." She added, "I'd rather be home cooking and cleaning, all those things I've been complaining about for 26 years. People say we need to prove ourselves . . ."

"If this is a test, I'm gonna fail," Spec. 4 Robin Williams was convinced. "A lot of other women are too, and I guess we're just going to have to accept that."[31]

Suzanne Fields, in a 1990 *Los Angeles Times* syndicated article, wrote:

Who will take care of the children? We should have
been planning for the chaos wreaked upon children
from the moment we said, "Yes, Mommy, you can be
a reservist, too, just like Daddy." So much that is said
on behalf of equal rights for women ignores the reality that babies need equal rights too.

Women have never before been so mercenary —
as to seek "rights" at the expense of their children. A
society that sends mommies off to participate in a war
when there is no actual military need to do so is a society that devalues its children.

How can it be possible that we have come to so
cheerfully sacrifice a child's right to a sense of well-
being, just to protect a woman's whim to prove that
she can make war as efficiently as a man?[32]

There seem to be no limits in satisfying such feminist
whims in Canada, which not only legislates women into all
the front lines of battle but also is the only country in the
world now legislating women into combat zones. (Nor-
way, the Netherlands and Belgium allow women to volunteer for the front lines, but invariably assign them to non-
combat zones.)

David Frum, an assistant editor of the *Wall Street Journal* and formerly a columnist for the *Toronto Sun*, explained in that Canadian newspaper that only through subversive tactics could such radical legislation have been
conceived. A three-person tribunal of the Canadian Federal
Human Rights Commission, composed of two lawyers and
one professor, none of whom had any military experience
or expertise whatever, had made the ruling — "arbitrarily,
capriciously, and ignorantly." Frum wrote:

The ten-day period they gave the armed forces to
make up its mind . . . fell, conveniently, while Parlia-

ment was prorogued, so that no M.P. could raise a question about what they had done. And by making sure the hearings were unpublicized, the commission was able to avoid hearing testimony from people who might disagree with the conclusion it intended to reach.

The tribunal claimed to have evidence that women could be put into combat units without impairing their ability to fight, but its evidence was inadequate, if not fraudulent . . .

Four nations have used women as soldiers in war: the Soviet Union, Yugoslavia, Israel and Sandinista Nicaragua. All four countries discovered that sexual integration is a disaster . . . and removed them from combat duty.

Women couldn't march as far or go without food as long as men. They couldn't carry as heavy a pack or throw a grenade as far. The camaraderie of soldiers under fire was shattered by sexual jealousy . . . when captured, female soldiers were more likely to be subject to atrocities by the enemy — and so their male comrades would often jeopardize the unit's other goals to keep them out of danger.[33]

Robert Stauffer, director of psychological research at the U.S. Military Academy at West Point, produces studies that prove female cadets have 30 to 40 percent less upper body strength than their male counterparts. Speed depends on strength, and so women run more slowly than the men. And because they have a lower concentration of red blood cells, which control cardiovascular capacity, women's performance in endurance events is inferior to that of men.[34]

Must we not take into account the fact that, in 1989, of 21 women who took the infantry tests at the Princess Patricia's Canadian Light Infantry Battle School at Wainwright, Alberta, only one was able to complete the course?[35]

Although aviation experts around the world agree with leading Danish military authorities that it is questionable whether a woman's body is able to take the punishing stress in the cockpit of a high-performance aircraft, Canada can now boast of having the first two women pilots in NATO to be assigned to fly jet fighters in combat.

There is a problem, however, in the extreme disapproval of male officers in the Canadian Air Command. A government survey indicated that 65.6 percent of fighter pilots are unwilling to work with female fighters, and a higher percentage of them will refuse to be supervised by them. "The mutual trust and cohesion so vital between a leader and his wingman could be missing in the male-female partnership," a male pilot explained.

Officers in all mixed combat units complain constantly of their forces being below strength, usually by at least 10 percent, because of the women on maternity leave.[36]

Democracy, fairness and justice seem to have been cast aside in North America as the complaints and wishes of a vast majority of citizens either are ignored or are censored under a now perfectly visible feminist dictatorship. If a referendum were held across the continent, it is doubtful that we would find more than a handful, apart from the interested parties, who would vote to put women on our warships. Indeed, our navies have the greatest difficulties filling the feminist-dictated quotas.

Canada's maritime commands reported it was impossible to attract the number of women they were ordered to assimilate into the crews of two of their ships, the *Nipigon* on the east coast and the *Provider* on the west coast. In the United States, the assigning of women to ammunition ships, oilers and other vessels in the navy's combat logistics force, expected to create 9000 new jobs for female sailors, is deeply resented by male personnel, whose years of seniority will no longer produce the promotions and pay raises they deserve.[37] Extreme rancor often exists between men and women on deck.

Or, there is "hanky-panky" on deck, as seen in the sensational news stories of steamy sex aboard the Coast Guard cutter *Rush*. In a court case, Lieutenant J. G. Christine Balboni and Chief Warrant Officer Charles Van Meter brought charges of harassment and sex discrimination against the crew. The captain of the *Rush* had accused the lieutenant of being "the sexpot of the wardroom"; and it was noted that the relationship between the accusers had caused the breakup of the warrant officer's marriage. Timothy Elledge, writing for United Press International, reported in the same story the testimony of witnesses describing the passionate romances in hidden rooms aboard ships, as well as the anger of navy wives ashore.[38] Navy wives, who have always been respected as a very special breed of women, keeping the home fires burning while their husbands serve their country on the seas, are now known to be particularly unhappy with the integration of women in the service. Some naval vessels already are nicknamed "the love boats."

Raising sensitive questions about the naval services' assimilation of women into all areas, a San Diego study, conducted through the San Diego Naval Hospital and released to the Associated Press in February 1988, documented some extremely alarming statistics: that 41 percent of pregnant sailors were unmarried; that 18 percent of that 41 percent were suffering from one of two different sexually transmitted diseases; that 38 percent of those women were still living on ships or in barracks and would have to be moved; and that 70 percent of them had decided to stay in the navy, despite having the option of resigning. The study recommended additional housing for women, quality child care facilities and access to pediatric medical care during evenings and weekends.[39]

"What do we have here now?" asked a retired admiral of the American fleet speaking to a group of civilians in the

San Diego area, "a great American naval fighting force — or a bunch of pregnant women and day care centers?"

The dramatic spread of the AIDS virus among women throughout the armed forces has been confirmed by Lieutenant Colonel John F. Brundage, chief of epidemiology at the Walter Reed Army Institute of Research, in a report stating: "Mandatory testing, since 1986, of American active duty army troops every two years and prior to being sent overseas, shows that the highest HIV infectivity rate by age for both sexes was in army women under 20 . . . and that approximately 50 percent of the infected females are married or have been married."[40]

While Pat Shroeder and other feminist leaders across the United States drive on toward ultimate androgyny in the military, and undoubtedly that would also include the Draft, they should think back some years. When President Jimmy Carter, under Betty Friedan's direction, brought in a bill that would have legislated all young women into the Draft, the women of America soundly defeated it.

In bringing men and women together again, in attempting to bring truth and justice back to our society, the women of the United States must again play an instrumental role in resisting the Draft. They must realize that the so-called discriminatory influence of male authorities does not deny women sexual equality, as feminist leaders would have us believe. At the same time, Canadian women must demand that "fraudulently" achieved feminist laws be rescinded. Two of these are: the assigning of women to combat units in the armed forces; and the forcing of all armed forces to accept the job applications of pregnant women. There are still no obstetricians assigned to Canadian warships.

The law forcing all Canadian armed forces to accept the job applications of pregnant women resulted from two highly publicized court cases, won by feminist lawyers, in which two pregnant women, in different branches of the military, were awarded damages for having been refused jobs. Cynthia Smith of Comox, British Columbia, received $1200 for lost wages and $700 for "injured feelings"; Marlene McAlpine of Ottawa accepted $4692 compensation, with an additional $700 for "injury to self-respect."[41]

Catherine Hoeck, a retired Belgian officer who served in NATO for six years, would discourage all young women who marry and have children from considering "the profession of arms." She was quoted in a newspaper interview as warning women against being in combat units particularly, "as they must be up to strength and ready to fight at all times." She recalled "a surprise midnight drill and a woman showing up with her two small children under her arms."[42]

MEN DENIED THEIR RIGHTS OF ASSOCIATION

It is time for women to realize how men are disadvantaged, how men are hurting, as feminists break up and break into all their formerly respected groupings, denying them their *rights of association.* The U.S. law guaranteeing freedom of association has long since been overridden by feminist legislation denying men that privilege.

In all areas of society feminist power, although successful in the "androgynizing" — the denaturalizing — of some women, has not been as effective in the neutering of men. However, I believe that by denying men their exclusive camaraderie, formerly assured in their close-knit associations — the armed forces and the men's clubs throughout North America, for example — their strengths have been dissipated. These very strengths might have resulted in a reasonable all-male resistance to the incredible injustices and the shocking imbalances imposed on society by feminist ideology.

There is no law in Canada guaranteeing freedom of association. Women's groupings multiply and multiply, and Amazonian feminists, forcing their will through feminist-influenced courts, forcing their presence into every traditionally male grouping, have successfully negated the constitutions of all public and private organizations; have destroyed an all-male camaraderie; and have denied men any *right* to group-determination.

Brian Mitchell, in his authoritative book *The Weak Link: The Feminization of the American Military*, published in 1989, discusses the loss of male camaraderie due to the increasing influx of women into all branches of the military; he considers it a most alarming threat to a nation's fighting capabilities. Many other military experts have expressed such views, citing the loss of such camaraderie as heading the list of handicaps imposed by feminism. (The list includes lighter weight guns, now produced for the women to carry.)[43]

It remains to be seen if the "androgynizing" of formerly all-male clubs and organizations will have as detrimental a long-term effect on society generally in the decline of services. In Canada, there is now an all-female Lions Club, with the power simply to address specific feminist goals; presumably, male members withdrew en masse.

The concerted feminist onslaught on men's organizations began bearing fruit in 1984, when a U.S. court order forced the Jaycees to accept female members. On May 4, 1987, after extremely costly court proceedings, the U.S. Supreme Court bowed to feminist pressure in ruling that Rotary International was guilty of discriminating by forbidding female members.[44]

Rotary, the oldest and most venerable men's organization, was founded in 1905 and has more than a million members in 161 countries around the world. When it was brought to its knees, other such clubs recognized the handwriting on the wall and, unwilling or unable to face the costly court cases to mount a defense of their own, have one by one succumbed to feminist demands. Kiwanis International with its 315,000 members worldwide must now allow women into all 8200 of its local organizations. The Lions Club International, boasting 1.3 million members, and Optimist International, with 160 North American groups, showed strong initial resistance but finally buckled under feminist pressures.

How ruthlessly resolved feminists are to bringing the whole male population into their androgynous mold is seen in their court proceedings against the Boys' Clubs of America (beginning in Denver), which succeeded in forcing the boys to accept girls into their rosters. Now, the wonderfully happy, positive programs arranged for boys by boys, which have kept thousands of boys from drifting into drugs or the street gangs, have been exchanged for new agendas that include dolls and day care. Boys' Clubs in many cities are disbanding, and no new ones are forming.

At the same time, there are millions of women's groups forbidden to men. In Canada, where injustices are most blatantly visible, there are all the federally funded, provincially funded women's councils, topped by the National Action Committee (NAC) in Ottawa, with the "action," I believe, aimed directly toward a feminist-socialist state. And there are the women's departments and courses at every university, where a raw brand of socialism — which levels men beneath their traditional, biological capabilities and raises women above theirs — is taught by acknowledged socialist leaders. A frosty welcome awaits any man who dares to intrude.

There are the all-female unions that will keep men out at all costs, such as the Federation of Women Teachers Association of Ontario. Although corresponding male unions, such as the Ontario Public School Teachers' Federation, have female members and female presidents and other officers, the women's union has in repeated court cases been successful in keeping out men.

Of course, there are the thousands of women's service

organizations across the continent, such as the Daughters of the American Republic (DAR), the Junior Leagues of America, and the Canadian IODE (Imperial Order Daughters of the Empire) and Women's Institute, that have long been active in improving the lives of men, women and children at home and abroad. Their members continue to treasure the lifelong friendships and close-knit "camaraderie" in their female-only groups that men were previously allowed to enjoy in their male-only groups.

Feminist lawyers have argued that men discuss business deals during club luncheons; now, women with a presence soon equaling that of men in the business world must also be offered the opportunities in such associations. (*Time* magazine, in its July 4, 1988, issue, predicted that women will dominate the business world by the year 2000.) However, men are simultaneously barred from corresponding women's groups, including the thousands of new women's networks that have sprung up in every city across the continent.

Recently, I spoke to one of several such prominent networks in the Toronto area. The 400 members call themselves "The Golden Girls," but their ages are between 20 and 50, and they are devoted to business and social interests — excluding men. In fact, in a question and answer period it became clear that few of the women, the majority of them extremely attractive, had any contact with any men other than their sons. I remembered that Roland Barthes, the famous French sociologist and lexicologist, had warned women in 1980 not to "back themselves into a *gynaeceum.*"

These women were certainly segregated into a *gynaeceum*, as in Greek and Roman eras, and there was a wistful, regretful note in a beautiful young woman's voice when she asked, "Why can't I 'connect' with a man? I meet someone I think could be a boyfriend and expect him to ask me out — but he doesn't. And then I notice he has that *wary* look in his eyes — as if I'm the cat and he's the mouse. Of course, I've noticed that look in the eyes of every man in our office. I don't think I'm a feminist, because I know women today are supposed to make all the first moves — but somehow, I just can't. I'm 32, and I think I'm a nice person, but I haven't had a date, even a 'let's go out for morning coffee date,' in four years. Do you know what's wrong?"

I suppose it has simply become too hard for many men to cross a battlefield with a Beirut lurking in every relationship; a Beirut that has been erupting since the very beginning of the Women's Liberation Movement in more than half the kitchens of North America and is still erupting; a Beirut in offices where pay equity, comparative worth and armies of enforcers impound the books and poison the very atmosphere between men and women; a Beirut that exploded in the absolute terror of the Montreal massacre: the death of 14 beautiful young female engineering students by a crazed fanatic — an ultimate, agonizing conclusion to the War of the Sexes.

BEIRUT ON THE CAMPUS

Although the horror of the Montreal incident has been generally dismissed as stemming from the mind of a madman, university administrators across North America are beginning to voice fears of a smoldering animosity that has been steadily building between men and women — perhaps rooted in the women's courses — with pressures as great and threatening to society as the San Andreas Fault is to the people of San Francisco.

There are reports of hundreds of minor incidents that indicate a growing animosity between men and women on university campuses. Male law students at the University of New Brunswick were forced to apologize for wearing T-shirts with the slogan, "He-Man Women-Haters Club."[45] At Queen's University in Kingston, Ontario, at the beginning

of the academic year, a poster campaign mounted by
women students, warning women of date-rape, outraged
male students who claimed it made all men out to be potential rapists. When a harassment officer was appointed at
the University of Toronto, with her substantial salary published in a year when the university was begging for
funds, one male student insisted, "she is simply going to
be prowling the campus — like a vampire, turning over
the stones, to find some poor jerk to accuse of harassment."

Barbara Amiel in an article in *Maclean's* magazine suggested that this may certainly have been the case when the
University of Toronto's Sexual Harassment Review Board,
composed of some obviously militant feminists, having
waited one full year for one single complaint, turned its
fury on a 60-year-old professor for "ogling" a 40-year-old
part-time student in a university swimming pool.

Professor Helen Rosenthal demanded the five-day hearing take place behind closed doors, no doubt foreseeing
the circus resulting from such a ridiculous charge, the disbelief and the uncontrollable laughter. Luckily her decree
was unheeded and the case, becoming a cause célèbre in
Canadian newspapers, illustrated exactly how far militant
feminists would go. Henceforth in Canada, *looking at a
woman* would become an indictable offense, and no
laughing matter.

The highly respected, long-tenured chemical engineering professor, Richard Hummel, was convicted and sentenced for "ogling" Beverley Torfason, only in the pool
and behind water goggles. She would seek $4000 in dam-
ages for stress. He would be found guilty and banished
from using that pool for five years, his former honorable
reputation sullied, his family injured and his health probably affected.

Barbara Amiel, in the *Maclean's* article, advised the University of Toronto to "borrow a set of stocks from its me-

dieval studies department so that its students may express
all that they have learned about life in the swimming pools
and on the playing fields of academe."[46] Jim Cormier in an
article in *Chatelaine* explained that "ogling" is purely a *human* impulse shared by both sexes; "more than one of
life's little pleasures — it's the bedrock of civilization as we
know it." Now, he wrote, "we guys often worry that wom-
en believe dark depravity lies behind the gaze of all men
— it has spelled death to the wolf whistle and the 'hey,
baby.'" Yet he points out that the wolf whistle and the
"overt surveillance" are very much alive when groups of
women all over the country gather for "cocktails and saucy
male burlesque performed by gifted gymnasts named
'Rugged Andy' and 'Long John Silver."[47]

While it would be a very foolish man who would dare
to swim in the University of Toronto's Hart House pool
while Ms. Torfason is doing her 40 lengths, it is ironic to
remember that Hart House itself, with all its sports and
recreation facilities, was built for and dedicated to the *men*
of the university by the Massey family (of the international
Massey-Ferguson firm) as a memorial to their son Hart,
who died in the First World War. (Another son, Vincent,
became a governor-general of Canada; another son is the
celebrated actor, Raymond Massey.) Long before the feminist pressures were applied, the men of the university had
enthusiastically welcomed women into a formerly happy
association in Hart House, where now its great halls are
filled with gloom as men and women pass one another
without speaking.

Bringing men and women together again on that campus is one of my particular aims, as I have several relatives
attending the university. It is also the yearning of the majority of men and women on that campus, according to a
random survey conducted in the months following the
Hummel conviction. No one was laughing, although several of the male undergraduates believed that all men should

now wear dark glasses for fear even a peripheral "look" could be construed as lascivious. The survey was to prove extremely important in its discovery that women were as incensed as the men by the outcome of the Hummel affair. Indeed, women made the greatest contributions to Professor Hummel's legal costs, in a fund initiated by Helen Barclay.

6

Stripping Away Feminism's False Faces

There are millions of lonely men and women pleading for love and companionship in the personal columns of newspapers throughout the Western world. There are countless dating services in all our cities, including cross-country computerized choices offered in video shops. Major hotel chains feature weekly dances for singles. There are also desperate and determined American men, paying thousands of dollars to bring European and Asian women to North America in arranged liaisons, who have simply given up all hope of the possibility of happiness with a North American mate in a feminist world.

Men and women are not *connecting* in a traditionally natural, normal fashion, according to studies of a significant phenomenon troubling society. They have been observed staring at one another across a dance floor, usually registering initial enthusiasm and hope, but later hostility, with women eventually dancing together in a high school gymnasium and men ducking out for beer in a nearby pub.

Television producer Irwin Patterson, acquainted with the scene, believes that the greatest efforts must be made to bring back the easy, trusting approaches of the past. He claims it is currently impossible to find or even recognize "a girl of one's dreams" behind the "feminist facade": the belligerent faces; the wary, untrusting faces; the downright fearful faces that say, "Could this pleasant-looking male really be one of those wolves in sheep's clothing?"

In a major newspaper article, Patterson wrote of the marriage and common-law legislation weighted so heavily against the male sex. He told of one close friend of his who, as insurance against economic disaster if the relationship was terminated, refused to live with his girlfriend for more than half of each week.[1]

There is no doubt that young men and young women are not "seeing" one another as they really are — usually decent, well-meaning human beings potentially of great promise — in their lives, in the community, in the world. Instead, they may "look" across that dance floor and "see" only the miserable images portrayed in feminist ideology, which I believe are rarely applicable to men.

In the early days of the Women's Liberation Movement, formerly knowledgeable, self-fulfilled and happy middle-class women had been persuaded that they were actually brainless, household slaves and drudges ("houseslugs" was the common word for them), and that they were oppressed and abused by husbands and employers. For many of them, breaking free meant denying their femininity — their inherent selfless, nurturing inclinations — to take on the new feminist image of a hard-driving, super-assertive individual calling all the shots, and cracking all the whips. (This is the image that many men apparently are still seeing across that dance floor.)

Of course, there were the role models of the movement — those women who rode roughshod over all traditional mores, determined to dominate and to impose their own feminist philosophy on governments and society generally. They were usually the most radical of the revolutionary protagonists, and included Germaine Greer, of the widest influence in Britain and Australia, who preached and promoted and demonstrated the sexual liberation that became a principal factor in the movement; Kate Millett, the avowed lesbian; and Gloria Steinem, founder and editor of *Ms*. The last two undoubtedly were the commanding forces in the United States, the former during her presidency of the National Organization of Women (NOW) and the latter as the founder and editor of the magazine that reaffirms feminist ideology in every issue. In Canada, Doris Anderson, for 17 years editor of the national women's magazine, *Chatelaine* — certainly the Canadian feminist manifesto during those years — and Louise Dulude, a president of the National Action Committee on the Status of Women (NAC), have proven what "hard-driving" and "belligerent" women can do. Dulude in 1989 was still demanding "a whole transformation of society in a most revolutionary way."[2]

However, the truth is, according to all comprehensive studies, that the majority of women throughout the Western world never fit into the radical feminist mold, nor did they deserve the ugly image. The American organization NOW never boasted more than 165,000 members (the 1990 claim),[3] and the Canadian NAC's published numbers claiming millions of members are consistently misleading: listed among the members are all members of the United Church of Canada and all members of such organizations as the YWCA. The tragedy is that the image of a dominant, vengeful feminist still clings like a pall over all women throughout the Western world, threatening the reconciliation of the sexes.

However, the image of the male portrayed in feminist ideology is nothing less than monstrous, and I am convinced that this picture has always been the trump card in the rise of feminism. Convincing women — convincing society — of the cruel and inhuman qualities in the male psyche has been the name of the game. This has been the weapon that, I believe, the feminists have used to whip up a terrible anger against men in the hearts of women particularly, and throughout society generally. Vengeance would naturally follow.

Mary Anne Dolan, editor of the *Los Angeles Herald Examiner*, in the June 1988 issue of the *New York Times* magazine, wrote: "Women's anger toward men is, I believe, even greater than before . . . Something is seriously askew."

Any fool knows that ever since Lucifer got loose in the Garden of Eden there have been male and female monsters in our world, and that we must recognize them and control them. However, when all media throughout our culture constantly, day by day, feature monstrous husbands abusing their wives, and monstrous boyfriends raping their girlfriends (80 percent of these cases are dismissed owing to convincing arguments that intercourse was invited by the girlfriend), surely we are seeing an organized campaign by radical feminist leaders, many of them controlling the media, to discredit all men.

Feminists can "rise on the backs of men only by showing that they are not fit to rule, by putting them down," according to my mother, who repeats over and over, "If you give a man a bad name, you may as well hang him." There is no doubt that men have been crushed and disarmed, persuaded of their collective crimes and burdened under their collective guilt.

When in headline after headline newspapers blazon so-called statistics that "Ten Percent of All Men [in Our Western Culture] Abuse Their Wives," no one bothers to point out that *90 percent of husbands are not abusing their wives*. And, I have found, the statistics are usually accepted from government-funded surveys conducted by rabid feminists. I have questioned those figures compiled by Linda McLeod in Canada, who lists her criteria as psychological, emotional and verbal as well as physical abuse, and who admits that her research is mainly taken from police files and women's shelters.[4]

An Advisory Council on the Status of Women, a government bureaucracy continually commissioning such studies, also deems abuse indictable if it has caused "a loss of dignity and control, a feeling of powerlessness."[5] Other studies define abuse as "pushing and shoving," but lawyers confirm the fact that husbands are constantly explaining that their "pushing and shoving" has been in self-defense, in avoiding the lethal weapons known to be used by wives in spousal attacks — iron frying pans, knives, axes and even fireplace pokers.

A particularly damning survey by Linda McLeod, commissioned by the Advisory Council, was publicized in a five-column-wide front-page article in a national newspaper (with a 700,000 paid circulation) carrying the screaming headline, "Anguish of One Million Women Reported." This 181-page study described the unbearable suffering of women — their depression, isolation and reduced life options — as a result of wife abuse, and it demanded unlimited funds to double the number of women's shelters across the country. It reported that in 1987, 42,000 women and 55,000 children had been cared for in 1100 units, often for several weeks at a time, and that 59 percent of the women eventually returned home to their former partners.[6] Critics of this study wondered how many women continually seeking such shelter had simply been "verbally" or "psychologically" abused — as in domestic disputes.

The shelters certainly fill an urgent need for physically abused women in our society, and in fact the need for similar retreats for men has now become apparent. Surveys show that in predivorce disputes and in the breakup of a relationship, in innumerable contested cases the man has been locked out, often unable to retrieve even a change of clothes. A professor of social work at the University of Wisconsin, R. L. McNeely, insists that reports on domestic violence should be fair and balanced and come from studies that examine the general population. Nicholas Davidson, in an article in the *National Review*, cites a number of studies, based on the general population, which indicate that women commit roughly as many assaults against spouses as men do. In the United States, 52 percent of spousal killings are by males and 48 percent by females, and hospitals report that approximately 250,000 men are seriously injured in spousal attacks and are admitted annually.[7]

While there is a never-ending litany throughout all media of the grimmest tales of wife abuse, the cases involving men, even seriously injured men, in spousal attacks are rarely publicized. Still, hundreds have been recorded. In Florida, a woman killing her husband with a headlock was not even charged — "it was simply the outcome of a domestic dispute."[8] In Ontario, a husband refused to take his wife to court although, following a "domestic dispute," she had poured a kettle of boiling water over him as he slept, permanently disabling him. In Winnipeg, Manitoba, a woman shot her common-law spouse in the back of the head during a drinking party and was unconditionally acquitted of murder (to her own surprise, she admitted).[9]

In 1990, the Supreme Court of Canada ruled that killing a husband is a perfectly legal act, without penalty, if there is "reasonable" proof that the husband had previously abused the wife.[10] Madam Justice Bertha Wilson, who wrote the "battered wife syndrome" decision, was given full credit for the ruling. Within a few months, Governor Richard Celeste of Ohio used Wilson's precedent to grant clemency to 25 women in Ohio prisons for murdering their husbands. Embittered men now suggest that there is an "open hunting season" on husbands, making marriage in itself a very dangerous option.[11]

The Toronto-based In Search of Justice Men's Organization, which is similar to many such organizations in Britain and the United States, may be unique in making "shelters for men" one of its goals. The organization, founded by its charismatic leader, Ross Virgin, has a dedicated membership throughout North America. Members from every level of society, many of them devastated in divorce proceedings and custody battles, or cruelly, unjustly disadvantaged in the workplace, often seek aid for individual justice.

The organization's endeavors are mainly unpublicized, and while members are continually attacked and reviled in all the media by feminists, and particularly in the talk shows, they have persevered in political lobbying to ensure legislation enforcing fathers' access rights, joint custody provisions in divorce settlements, grandparents' rights, and a ban on the publication of the names of men accused of child abuse unless convicted.

Ross Virgin believes that women who fraudulently charge husbands with child abuse to obtain child custody should themselves face the stiffest penalties. He says: "This weapon has become one of the most sadistic, underhanded, back-stabbing tools which women have decided to use against their husbands during and after a divorce."[12]

Robert Wakefield, president of the Canadian Association of Criminal Defence Lawyers, testified:

Men are blackmailed into settling marital disputes by the mere threat of child sexual abuse charges. It has become the weapon of choice . . . in domestic disputes. You merely have to point the finger at an offending spouse . . . and they are vaporized. They may as well be from Mars in terms of their Rights in court hearings . . . the legislation a blueprint for convictions.[13]

Rob Nicholson, a prominent Niagara Falls lawyer and Member of Parliament, told a parliamentary committee that if a client of his were charged with child sexual abuse, he would tell him to start "selling his property and move to another part of the country."[14]

The Children's Aid Society in Toronto has reported that, of the charges of sexual abuse of children leveled at fathers in the divorce cases in which the society was involved during a 12-month period, 95 percent were unfounded. Continent-wide statistics show that fathers have been proven innocent in 95 percent of all sexual abuse cases.[15] Ontario Judge Ted Matlew, in acquitting one man, regretted that "taxpayers are being put to needless expense, and the courts clogged by the sexual-assault trials that are clearly a waste of time."[16]

Furthermore, there are constant statistics that prove women commit two-thirds of all child abuse, and that "most of this abuse is committed in households headed by a single female."[17]

It is also a fact that the majority of wife abuse charges are unfounded. Peter Jaffe, director of the London, Ontario, Family Court Clinic, stated that "only one out of every 250 so-called wife-abusers is ever convicted of the offense."[18] In Chicago, 10 years after he was convicted on rape and kidnapping charges and sentenced to 25 years in prison, Gary Dotson had those charges dropped when the woman who had accused him recanted her testimony.[19] Are men, simply because they are men, still in the gravest danger of being convicted in such cases?

The thousands of cases in which men are proven innocent are never reported, although the false testimonies, either general or specific, continually appear in all media. Feminism seems to have triumphed over groveling men.

When a front-page article in newspapers declared in a giant headline that "One in Five Jewish Wives Is Battered by her Husband — Violence Hits Jewish Families," Barbara

Harris, director of Transition Center in New York City, stated flatly: "That is simply not true."[20]

At a government-funded women's conference in Ottawa in the spring of 1988, which featured lesbian workshops and a woman-only dance, attending feminists were selling lapel buttons that read: "The Only Good Man Is a Dead One."[21]

I believe we have been dominated in legislation and influenced in every area of society by such monstrous lies and by the false premises of feminist ideology. I also believe that men and women, by seeing one another without feminism's false faces, will bring down other barriers.

It is time for men and women to deny the lies and begin to see one another again as they really are — not as they have been portrayed for the purposes and power of radical feminism.

MEN AND WOMEN: THE TRUE IMAGES

Men are magnificent — when they train their minds and bodies and emotions in a lifetime of effort to walk on the moon, and then stroll across that wondrous landscape, singing, in a great, joyous upsurge of the human spirit, "We were strolling in the park one day."

Men are giants — such as Mikhail Gorbachev and Lech Walesa, who shouldered a whole Eastern world beyond the social and economic failures of Communist ideology.

Men are heroes — the millions of them who, with the courage of lions, lived and died in a sea of blood on all those battlefields in our modern wars — beating back the Hitlers and the evils that would have engulfed us, many of the survivors coming home to endure a lifetime of physical and mental pain.

Men are godly — armies of men who, with the purest motives and inspired commitment in aiding mankind, are still following Albert Schweitzer into the darkest, most despairing areas on earth.

Men are selfless — as was witnessed when a man escaped from the wreckage of a plane in Sioux City, Iowa, in the summer of 1989, only to climb back and grope his way through blinding smoke to answer the wail of an infant he was able to save.

Men are statesmen — despite a jaundiced public view, the largest percentage of politicians may be recognized as public servants of scrupulous honesty and high ideals.

Men are geniuses — Moses and Dante and Shakespeare and Milton originating our thought and morality.

Men are noble husbands — "great of character," they have devoted their vision, strengths, courage and honor to their wives and families from time immemorial, a prerogative that would now be denied them in feminist ideology. (We know marriage will never be perfect, but even full of conflict and problems, the ordinary vicissitudes of daily life, it promises stability, safety and elemental joys to be found nowhere else in human experience.)

Men are human beings — with the frailties of all humankind.

Real women are human beings with all the frailties of humankind. They are neither "brainless drudges" who care for their own beloved children at home, nor are they denaturalized females cloning men in the workplace — as feminism has conceived them.

Real women are magnificent, with many of the attributes
of men, but with added grace and with the power to hold
destiny — the beginning or the ending of civilization —
within the womb. The greatest women leaders of all times
have never denied that maternity is the pivotal center of a
woman's existence; only the modern feminist leaders have
dared to do so.

The Holy Mother is worshipped as the abiding symbol
of motherhood. Mother Theresa "mothers" the world's
poor. Margaret Thatcher considered homemothers of
paramount importance to the society that she rescued from
economic doom. Golda Meier could never be recruited to
the Women's Liberation Movement; she asked: "Feminists?
Are they those crazy people who burn bras?"

I believe that former American feminist leaders and such
role models as Nellie McClung in Canada would have dis-
sociated themselves from modern feminist ideology, which
has resulted in the alienation of the sexes, the destruction
of traditional family lifestyles and the abandonment of children. It was the social issues of those earlier times, specifically slavery and alcoholism, that motivated women to become involved in public affairs and have a voice in government. In their philosophy, being able to address such
problems on a community level was simply an extension
of a woman's family concerns and caring nature.

McClung, a prolific writer of books and articles who in
1918 was appointed by Prime Minister Sir Robert Borden
to the Canadian War Conference, later became influential
as a member of the Alberta legislature and a champion of
all family-oriented causes, including public health, rural
improvements and, particularly, temperance. The family,
"the mothering ideal, were central to McClung's feminism
. . . She regarded motherhood as the highest achievement
of her sex," wrote Veronica Strong-Boag in her biographical introduction to a 1972 edition of McClung's *In Times
Like These.*[22]

Phyllis Schlafly's efforts to save "the mothering ideal" and traditional morals and family lifestyles in the United States may have actually rescued a whole civilization as we have known it from possible extinction, and I believe her work will earn her more than the accolades she receives annually in the press as "one of the most influential women of our times."

I am convinced that she will go down in all history books throughout the Western world as "the most influential woman of *all* times," with the stature of a Churchill. No American can deny that Schlafly's leadership and efforts stopped ERA, the Equal Rights Amendment, from being passed. (Women in every state still wear her STOP ERA buttons.) The final "No" votes proved that the majority of Americans, male and female, were behind her, growing more dedicated every year to her principal goals of "saving the family" and bringing back the moral values that had built a great nation.

A homemother who taught her six children to read before they went to school, and a Harvard graduate who received her J.D. from the Washington University Law School, she is a member of the Administrative Conference of the United States (a federal panel of law experts) and has testified before hundreds of congressional and state legislative committees.[23]

The *Phyllis Schlafly Report*, which she launched in 1967, reaches thousands of her supporters throughout every state, politically activating remarkable women (who in turn begin to lead others) with her minute instructions. "Write your Congressman today — and here is *his* name. Know the Congressmen — here are *their* names — who voted for the Bills that will enforce Pay Equity that would destroy the working potential of your husbands and fiancés; that would allow abortion on demand, to decimate our race; that would corrupt our children by putting condoms in the hands of five-year-olds; that would bring in Universal Day

Care, driving all mothers from their homes and children —
and DEFEAT THEM." She has convinced the women of
America that only in federal and state legislation can they
turn back the feminist tide that threatens the sanctity of
marriage and families.

Her Eagle Forum, which was incorporated in 1975 to receive donations for her nationwide efforts, was named for
the creature that mates for life. Founded originally as an
offshoot of the National Federation of Republican Women
(NFRW), of which she had been a vice president, the Eagle
Forum has become a powerful, vocal grass-roots coalition
of "Republicans and Democrats, urban Catholics and
Southern fundamentalists, Mormons and Orthodox Jews,
blue-collar ethnics and white-collar suburbanites"[24] who
could overcome ERA to fight on other fronts.

Across the nation, members fight to reform a desperately flawed educational system in a country that spends
more on education per capita than any other country in
the world. They would bring back the moral teaching of
the old *McGuffey Readers*, which "taught the time-honored
virtues: love of God, patriotism, thrift, honesty, respect for
elders, where there's a will there's a way, the Golden Rule,
true courage, manliness, kindness to the less fortunate,
obedience to parents, the value of prayer, the consequences of idleness and truancy, crime doesn't pay, and
why virtue and love are worth more than material
riches."[25]

This teaching would replace the current Humanist
guidelines published in the *Second Humanist Manifesto* in
1973, under the sponsorship of Betty Friedan and John
Dewey, that deny God and Bible teaching, leaving little
children particularly with the awesome responsibility of
deciding themselves what is right or wrong.[26]

"Feminine" women — dedicated wives and mothers and
young future wives and mothers — hail Phyllis Schlafly as
"the best thing since Joan of Arc."[27]

In Britain, Valerie Riches is another Joan of Arc, also determined to change a society where, she believes, sex education throughout the educational system has led directly to many of the social problems caused by "the ravages of permissiveness." Her book, *Sex and Social Engineering*, analyzes the radical influences "which gave rise to escalating figures of divorce, one-parent families, children in care of local authorities, illegitimacy, abortion, venereal disease and the many other emotional and physical manifestations of human distress."[28] As an Oxford-trained sociologist working with unmarried mothers, she had come face-to-face with all such distress.

In addition to writing and to lecturing throughout Europe, Australia, Africa and North America, she has been the driving force of the prestigious Family and Youth Concern Organization (formerly the Responsible Society) since becoming its secretary in 1972. Her husband, Denis Riches, formerly one of Britain's foremost industrialists, joined her in the founding of a publishing house that produces numerous books and pamphlets and a newsletter devoted to bringing back the morality and strengths of the traditional nuclear family. Critics have predicted that their 1991 anthology, *Feminism v. Mankind*, will top British bestseller lists. Their videos, including one about "morality v. AIDS," which are produced by their associate, Robert Whelan, have been purchased by the British navy to be shown on all training ships and are distributed throughout educational systems.

As seen in the support and influence of other prominent educators and writers, such as Christine M. Kelly, Josephine Robinson, Sir Bryan Thwaites (former principal of Westfield College, University of London) and Baroness Diana Elles (who was raised to the peerage after a distinguished five-year term as vice president of the European Parliament and now sits on the influential European Select Committee), British society is experiencing a reawakening to a new age. The family, with all its former moral values, may again become the heart and might of a great nation.

In Canada, REAL WOMEN was the name chosen by another inspired Joan of Arc, Gwendolyn Landolt, for an organization she founded that is composed of women dedicated to preserving the family and to halting the erosion of all moral values. Landolt was a lawyer as well as an accomplished writer who, having given up a prestigious career in government law to raise her five children, became increasingly concerned about the desperate problems of so many other children.

She was preparing dinner one night in 1983 when she heard on the radio that the federal government intended to remove a tax exemption for dependent, at-home spouses so that more money could be channeled into public day care, and her concern was galvanized into action. She saw this policy as a design to drive more women out of their homes, encouraging them to abdicate the care of children and husbands. This would eventually undermine marriages and deny children the security of formerly happy and stable lifestyles.

Landolt, with a few telephone calls to concerned friends, launched REAL WOMEN that dinner hour and within two years 50,000 women across Canada had joined up to voice their concern. In every province, women, led by other extremely talented women — prominent journalist Doreen Beagan in Prince Edward Island, Lettie Morse in Ottawa, Cecilia Forsyth in Saskatchewan, Lorna LaGrange in Alberta, Peggy Steacy in British Columbia and so many others — were realizing the need to organize, to influence the laws, to save families.

Of course, it was to be expected that feminist opposition to such an organization would be more virulent in Canada than in the United States or Britain. While feminist writers regularly reviled and ridiculed the members, calling them "dowdy, dinosaurs — living in another age," all media, obviously feminist-dominated, ignored the organization's news releases.

REAL WOMEN found it hard to believe that the federal government would deny members any funds to carry on their countrywide creative efforts to "Save the Canadian Family"; to bring back respect for the homemother, while still allowing women all choices; and to ensure fair taxation for all parents — the organization's continuing platforms. In one desperate attempt to gain the attention of Parliament, they took batches of homemade muffins into the House of Commons (borrowing an early Phyllis Schlafly tactic).

Women throughout the Western world, I believe, are realizing how slow we all have been in understanding exactly what has been happening to society generally as a result of the feminist ideology that has insidiously permeated all levels of governments and all levels of our educational system. The billions of taxpayers' dollars spent on women's councils, women's committees, women's conferences, and women's studies courses and departments have certainly taken women out of the mainstream — away from men and children, divorced from "The Family."

REAL WOMEN are convinced that men and women and children should be together again in the mainstream, facing social issues as a family; that the thousands of women's councils and committees and conferences should be designated *family* councils and committees and conferences; and that all the study courses and departments in the universities should be for women and men.

Men and women were put on this earth *together*, and belong *together*. Of course they do, and they must begin to see one another again in true perspective. Men must see the real women — divinely feminine — not the denaturalized feminists who grow long in the tooth and more radical with age. And women must surely begin to *see* men again, not as "male chauvinist pigs" so condemned in femi nist ideology, but as generally good and well-meaning human beings. There are more than "A Few Good Men" (the title of the most popular play on Broadway in 1990).

Then, attracted to one another, loving one another, *together again*:

There may be dancing in the streets,
As another wall comes crumbling down,
And banners,
And joy, as men and women meet
Again, in trust,
And the armistice is signed,
And broken hearts are whole.

PART
II
Love and Sex

One who loves looks on the face of God.
Valjean, in Victor Hugo's *Les Miserables*, 1862

Science is a mere trifling
nothing is real but love
Pierre Simon, *Marquis de la Place*, one of the world's earliest and
greatest astronomers; in Paris, on his deathbed, 1826

7
Rock and Romance
— and the Roots

Love is of the mysteries of the spirit and the subtleties of the mind, while sex may be said to spring from the elemental core of the physical being. When the two come together with the will and strength to endure in harmony in the union of a man and a woman, then, so the poets and the philosophers have told us, men and women may indeed reach for the sublime.

Yet it would seem that love and sex could finally be totally disconnected in our modern culture, which has succumbed to all the principles of women's "liberation." Such "principles" have included giveaway love and the permissive satiation of sex; and, from the very beginning, rock music has been exploding with the messages.

Myrna Kostash in her book *Long Way from Home* wrote about the earlier days of rock and roll and described Bob Dylan's "apocalyptic vision of a world depleted of order, habit and convention . . . that saw us all accepting, 'this grotesque and suffering self these songs make us an offering of . . .'"[1]

Madonna, Bruce Springsteen, Michael Jackson and the rest have been the conduits, the voices expressing our times, our woes, our wild extremes throughout these years of "liberation." Scraps of their songs keep crowding through our consciousness.

Madonna, becoming the personification of raw, uninhibited sex in her world concert tours, glorifies the one-night stands, and "the physical attraction," that is no more than "a chemical reaction . . . we can't take it anywhere."

Bruce Springsteen sings of a "death trap . . . a suicide rap."

Michael Jackson reaps a fortune every time he steps before his multitude of fans, screaming out his sad tales of soulless sex ("Dealing out the agony within . . . and no one's giving in . . ."); still, one song talks of a "willow deeply scarred, Somebody's broken heart, And a washed-out dream."

But it is Corey Hart who would "capture all the love the great romantics had, Sing you a song that ain't half bad — But that ain't enough."

Still, in 1989, almost in answer to Hart's wistful yearning, B. B. King and the You Too's were famous again, bringing back their songs of gentle love, of healing love, of mother love. ("No one loves me but my mother," he sings at San Quentin, where he performs regularly and is named an "honorary inmate.") And there are indications that many other great modern minstrels who pack auditoriums are ready to revamp their material and rescue that "washed-out dream" and bring back "the love the great romantics had."

Looking back, it may not be seen as anything less than a tragedy: women, in their mass exodus from their homes during those early years of the Women's Liberation Movement, also left behind the romantic concept of love — exchanging the bonding of love and sex for the treacherous waters of sexual liberation. Throughout the centuries women had been the inspiration for such romantic love; now they were abandoning it. At the same time, many men were learning to overcome their distaste for "loose" women, as they were once called. These events would herald the new era of free copulation.

Revolutionary thought — certainly revolutionary to the women of North America — would insist that sexuality as the predominant force in human nature be as open as the flowers in the field, no longer to be smothered under moral disciplines that feminists contemptuously labeled the "Victorian code." In all our relationships and in our lifestyles, our sexuality would be offered free rein, unhindered by law or any other social restraints.

The United Church of Canada, the largest Protestant denomination in the country, would actually condone such sexual freedom as the normal behavior of our times. It did so in a major statement of policy in 1988. Children in the lowest grades were already being told about "natural" permissible sexuality, while older ones, but as young as 12, would be welcoming the condom machines in school washrooms. Where was love? What was love?

Anyone could see that love had long ago become divorced from sex. The word "love," of course, would come to be misused, particularly by younger men and women who were often longing to add "something" to an empty, unsatisfying sexual experience. The stunning young woman, a little bit tipsy in a hotel bar, who said "I could love you" to a handsome stranger, was offering a one-night stand.

A very old grandmother of mine claimed she knew "what was love." On her 70th wedding anniversary to "that cranky old wreck of a man," whom she obviously loved so dearly, she said: "Love can be a tiny flame, and you must fan it every single day of your lives together. Sometimes there are horrible things that happen and threaten to blow it out; sometimes it almost putters out; and sometimes it could light Times Square. But usually it is simply a steady glow — and you come to realize that, without it, you would be groping in the dark." (As it happened, Grandma died at 92, only a few months after Grandpa, who died at 99.)

I heard Jane Fonda on a television interview say: "I can't imagine what it would be like to grow old without someone to love you." But now Fonda is divorced again, as are so many of our friends and neighbors.

"Old-fashioned" love demanded permanence, or at least the expectation of permanence. It would be in this expectation that love would root, joining two lives. Lifetime aspirations would be interwoven — slowly, and sometimes laboriously. Only in a determined commitment in marriage could a man and woman gain the strength to grow and endure together, accepting all the ordinary vicissitudes that happen in all our lives, the disappointments, the disenchantments, and the suffering, yet triumphing in exquisite joys.

Nor would their singular "identities" ever be lost, as the feminists have consistently claimed they would be, with the wife simply becoming a servile vassal under the husband. Instead, a husband and wife, growing closer and closer, instinctively draw on each other's strengths to enhance their individual stature. As far as the female partner being the vassal, I have never observed a loving marriage in which the wife was not, quite obviously, the team manager, as well as the nurturer and the comforter of both husband and children.

Antoine de Saint-Exupery, in *Wind, Sand and Stars*, wrote: "Love does not consist in gazing at each other but in looking outward together in the same direction."

THE ROOTS

The destruction of such "love," the severing of love and sex, began with the direct assault of socialist theory and the rise and success of communism in the East. However, it would take almost a century for the concept to permeate Western thought before exploding in North America through the Women's Liberation Movement.

The 19th-century British philosopher and politician, John Stuart Mill, was probably the first political voice to insist that freeing women from the "bondage of marriage" must be the first step to a vastly improved social order.

Mill's powerful essay, *The Subjection of Women*, was written in 1861 and published in 1869, when he admitted that its driving principles were those of Harriet Taylor, certainly a domineering and dedicated feminist, who had been his constant companion for 20 years before becoming his wife. (When Mill married Taylor in 1851, he made a public declaration "against the existing law of marriage.")

The essay dealt with women as the "subject class": women subtly and pervasively conditioned by society to be the slaves of men within the traditional marriage structure:

> The family is a school of despotism, within which the virtues of despotism, but also its vices, are largely nourished . . . All women are brought up from the very earliest years in the belief that their ideal of character is the very opposite to that of men . . . All the moralities tell them that it is the duty of women, and all the current sentimentalities that it is their nature to live for others.[2]

The present hate and vengeance and revulsion toward men, such a major component in the feminist revolution of our times, may have been sparked in that essay. Speaking of their "mean and savage natures," Mill wrote:

> If the family in its best forms is, as it is often said to be, a school of sympathy, tenderness, and loving for-

getfulness of self, it is still oftener, as respects its
chief, a school of wilfulness, overbearingness, un-
bounded selfish indulgence, and a double-dyed and
idealised selfishness . . .

It would be tiresome to repeat the commonplaces
about the unfitness of men in general for power,
which, after the political discussions of centuries,
everyone knows by heart.[3]

Not only did the essay ignore moral values and the
physical security that are the great strengths of the family
structure, but it also attempted to tear away all spiritual
considerations. The essay played a significant role in shap-
ing the atheistic views that would lead to the formation of
the socialist state and later find their place in feminist philosophy.

I believe that the Mill essay, which had such an overwhelming influence throughout the world, providing the
principal thesis in feminist ideology, should have lost all
credibility simply on the basis of the author's lack of
knowledge on the matter of differences between the sexes:

. . . what are the natural differences between the two
sexes — a subject on which it is impossible in the
present state of society to obtain complete and cor-
rect knowledge — while almost everybody dogma-
tises upon it . . .

The profoundest knowledge of the laws of the formation of character is indispensable to entitle anyone
to affirm even that there is any difference, much
more what the difference is, between the two sexes
considered as moral and rational beings; and since no
one, as yet, has that knowledge (for there is hardly
any subject which, in proportion to its importance,
has been so little studied), no one is thus far entitled
to any positive opinion on the subject. Conjectures

are all that can at present be made.[4]

Sigmund Freud was one of the few prominent Europeans to criticize severely Mill's assessment of the male and female roles in marriage and in society generally. He was convinced that Mill's essay simply lacked understanding of the male and female temperaments.

Of course, it was only after Mill had gained fame as a powerful parliamentary ally in the British Women's Suffrage Movement that *The Subjection of Women* was published and became well-known, with the most far-reaching results. His amendment to the 1867 Reform Bill had been largely responsible for women's enfranchisement in Britain, although evolutionary events (as described in my book, *The Feminist Takeover*), including the increasing ownership of property by women, had set the stage.

In North America, the rooted commitment to the ideal of associating sex with love, and to the concept of fidelity and permanence within monogamous marriage, seemed unshakable — until the rise of a philosophy called "Humanism." Spelled out by Dr. Brock Chisholm in *Can People Learn to Learn*, this ideology proved a deadly weapon in an assault on the traditional North American family.

Chisholm, who believed in world government and in the state's right to manipulate society, became the first director of the World Health Organization and, later, the president of the World Federation for Mental Health, positions in which he had extensive opportunities to promote Humanist philosophy.

He would develop and put forward the theory that, to establish a more civilized way of life throughout the world, all concepts of "right and wrong" had to be eliminated, denying religious and other cultural restraints. He blamed parents specifically for repressing their offspring's "natural" sexuality, and he insisted that sex education be introduced in the schools by the fourth grade. It is Chisholm who is now credited with the establishment of sex education throughout school systems.[5]

Later, the permissive sexual behavior he endorsed in Humanism would be supported in the 1948 and 1953 Kinsey Reports that were financed by the Rockefeller Foundation. The studies indicated that there was no such thing as "rights and wrongs" or "normal or abnormal" in sexual behavior. And while the subjects of the studies had been volunteers and not a sampling from the general population, inviting skepticism from the scientific community, the media's exploitation of the sensational data was successful in drowning out all criticism.[6]

Still, the moral values and strengths in the preservation of the traditional North American family held firm for a while, and the general attitudes toward sexual liberation did not give way. Then, in the sixties, Betty Friedan's book *The Feminine Mystique* suddenly found the Achilles' heel of the women of North America.

This was in her direct attack on their own self-esteem, their self-image, their self-worth. As homemakers, their incalculable contributions to local and world communities through magnificent devotion to families and volunteer work as well — would lie in ashes at their feet, denigrated beyond recall.

The radical feminist leaders immediately recognized the Achilles' heel that Friedan may have inadvertently exposed. Middle-class women across the continent, smarting unbearably under the feminists' disparaging epithets of "houseslug," "drudge," "slave," "waster of talent" or "brainless echo of a mother's past," would be persuaded to leave all they had formerly held dear — their husbands, their children, their homes — often for dull one-dimensional jobs in the workplace.

As men and women grew further and further apart, love and sex in a new culture would disengage, with intercourse often looked forward to simply as a clinical connection: without spontaneity, without trust, without heart, without soul and without any true meaning.

Alexander Solzhenitsyn, the great Russian religious activist and writer, now on our shores studying the overwhelming distress in our society, has asked: "How did the West decline from its triumphal march to its present sickness?" He would attempt to answer that question himself in a major article that appeared in *Time* magazine:

> There is technical progress, but this is not the same thing as the progress of humanity as such. In Western civilizations — which used to be called Western-Christian but now might better be called Western-Pagan — along with the development of intellectual life and science, there has been a loss of the serious moral basis of society . . . When Western society was established . . . everyone understood what he could do and what he could not do. Since then, the only thing we have been developing is rights, rights, rights, at the expense of duty.[7]

OUR CHILDREN, OUR FUTURE

All our hopes of recovery, of course, rest with our children, and our greatest efforts must be on their behalf. How could we have imagined the terrible consequences that this "sweeping away" of "the serious moral basis of society" would have on children?

We know we cannot turn back the clock. At best, we can ease the discomfort and the suffering of victims of the feminist revolution: the despair of the divorced, the loneliness of the singles, the pain of people with AIDS. So many were persuaded that divorce, the single cult and unleashed promiscuity are norms in our society. But it cannot be too late to rescue our children — our babies, our preschoolers, our elementary schoolchildren, our sophisticated teenagers — from all such persuasion.

Right now, our children have little conception of the meaning of true love — of the mystical involvement of the spirit that may sanctify the physical passion. There are no classes teaching teenagers all the advantages of permanent love — the simple decency, respect, chastity, responsibility and dignity that can glorify the conjugal act.

Instead, our school systems across North America are inundated with explicit sex education, giving children the knowledge and a license to destroy themselves, emotionally and physically. Sex education in the schools condones "safe" sexual expression from the earliest ages and has resulted in more than half of all North American teenagers engaging in early, uninhibited sex.

In these past decades of the feminist revolution, parents, it would seem, have abdicated from all their responsibilities. Formerly the primary educators of their own children, they exercised the right to instill in them their own values, morals, attitudes and religious beliefs. Today, parents have given carte blanche to the educational systems and to television, as well as allowing these influences to establish all standards of social behavior for the kids of our liberated society.

There simply may be too many mothers seeking their own identities, their interests concentrated principally outside the home, who fail to recognize the increasing psychological and physical dangers that their children are exposed to within the school systems. More than that, because half of all marriages end in divorce and fathers lose their children in 85 percent of all custody cases, there is a very large percentage of fathers without any influence in the parenting of their children.

At the same time, teachers have been effectively hamstrung in many of their efforts to restore any traditional values. They have been forbidden to use prayers, a simple method of touching the spiritual in the mind of a child and providing a nourishing respite in the midst of a harried school agenda. Throughout the school systems across the continent, teachers are not even allowed to suggest the advantages — the love and care and tenderness — that may be found in a traditional family.

Dr. Paul C. Vitz in his government study found that the "family" is no longer given credence in public school textbooks, with the very words "marriage, husband, and homemaker" now taboo.[8]

Little girls are no longer to see themselves as future mothers, but only as slicked-up career types working shoulder to shoulder with the feminized, desexualized male. At the same time they are being taught that their "natural" sexuality need not be denied, with in-school instructions on condoms and the Pill. They are fully aware of the alternatives as well: abortion, or government support if they decide to go ahead with a teenage pregnancy. There is no doubt that they have learned to accept promiscuity as a norm in observing some of their mothers, aunts and sisters, and from watching unrestrained lust on television any night of the week.

Dr. Margaret White, the eminent British gynecologist, was quoted in medical journals throughout the world when she advised teenagers of the dangers in early use of the Pill:

> If you give girls the Pill before they are totally physically mature, they risk, first, interference with their normal growth; second . . . they are more likely to develop diabetes; third, they may never develop regular periods. They may get depression. It should never be given to anyone under 17. *Never.*[9]

Nevertheless, sex education programs throughout our school systems — and society generally — seem to be handing our children something akin to dynamite.

The serious risk in teaching and enforcing the feminist

theory of androgyny — the equality of the sexes — recently came to light. Day in and day out, in sports and in classes, male and female children plainly see the differences that they are no longer allowed to acknowledge. (No handicap programs have been able to overcome the male predominance in mathematics and science, for example.) Boys have reason to complain that their inherent sense of initiative and traditional skills are continually downgraded.

Psychologists have discovered that male children under such constraints are failing to define their future role — reflecting the dilemma of modern, confused men in our society. Teenage boys watch the steamy free sex on television and take in such movies as *The War of the Roses*, where the battles of married couples escalate into near-murder. So they may decide to go for the free sex, but not for the marriage. If little girls are no longer encouraged to see themselves as future wives and mothers, then boys may no longer see themselves as future loving husbands and fathers.

Our children may never regain the sweetness and serenity of lost innocence, but we can teach them that they may find the happiness all human beings seek. We can teach them this by bringing love and marriage together again; by once more aspiring to courtship, marriage and commitment.

Ted Koppel, moderator of TV's *Nightline,* addressed the graduating class of Duke University in Durham, North Carolina:

> We have actually convinced ourselves that slogans will save us. Shoot up if you must, but use a clean needle. Enjoy sex whenever and with whoever you wish, but wear a condom. No!
>
> The answer is No. Not because it isn't cool or smart or because you might end up in jail or dying in

an AIDS ward, but No because it's wrong, because we have spent 5,000 years as a race of rational human beings, trying to drag ourselves out of the primeval slime, by searching for truth and moral absolutes.

In its purest form, truth is not a polite tap on the shoulder. It is a howling reproach. What Moses brought down from Mount Sinai were not *The Ten Suggestions.*[10]

8

Sexual Warfare

Men must understand that the sexual warfare which women began to wage against them in the early days of the Women's Liberation Movement was not instigated by the majority of women across North America. This warfare was simply the ultimate strategy devised by the most brilliant of feminist protagonists in a revolution that could denaturalize men and women and create an androgynous society.

In the forefront of the campaign, of course, would be the most powerful lesbian leader, Kate Millett, whose book, *Sexual Politics*, demanded a revolution to ensure a new "sexual order." She wrote of a "cultural revolution, which, while it must necessarily involve the political and economic reorganization traditionally implied by the term revolution, must go far beyond this as well . . ."[1]

The author's seemingly obsessive hatred of men and contempt for the wife and motherhood role sprang from every page. Men were depicted as the monstrous oppressors of women in a patriarchy that must be completely dismantled, beginning with the destruction of its institutional roots — marriage and the family. Marriage, Kate Millett claimed, was basically a financial arrangement, with a woman forced economically into becoming a sexual slave and domestic servant, "in the position both of minor and chattel throughout her life. Her husband became something like a legal keeper, as by marrying she succumbed to a mortifying process which placed her in the same class with lunatics or idiots . . ." [2]

The family, which has provided the lifeblood and strength of nations, she saw as irredeemably corrupt; parents were unfit to raise their own children — they were "too frequently unhappy persons with little time nor taste for the work." She predicted that Universal Day Care would be successful in hastening the final demise of the family. Ridding society of marriage and the family, she said, would create "a world we can bear, out of the desert we inhabit."

It seems inconceivable that her lesbian approach, separating men from women, love from sex, women from children, without an indication of any understanding about the minds and hearts of men and women, could have been accepted by her readers. When she wrote, "The concept of romantic love affords a means of emotional manipulation which the male is free to exploit,"[3] readers may have wondered if she knew anything of the romantic vulnerability existing in the male psyche, which not incidentally, women exploit today.

A tirade of articles by radical feminist writers in the anthology *Sisterhood Is Powerful*, edited by Robin Morgan, dwelt on the same themes:

Romance, like the rabbit at the dog track, is the illusive, fake, and never-attained reward which for the benefit and amusement of our masters keeps us running and thinking in safe circles.

A relationship between a man and a woman is no

more or less personal a relationship than is the relationship between a woman and her maid, a master and his slave . . .

. . . the family has fallen apart . . . the family unit is a decadent, energy-absorbing, destructive wasteful institution for everyone except the ruling class . . . collective action among women is fast destroying the decadent family ideology along with its ugly individualism and competitiveness and complacency. Our demand for collective public child care is throwing into question the private family (or individual ownership) of children.[4]

Shulamith Firestone, in her book *The Dialectic of Sex*, published in 1970 and still avidly read in the women's studies courses, preached about "the freeing of women from the tyranny of their biology by any means available . . . Childbearing could be taken over by technology." Apparently she considered the mating of a man and woman a loveless, meaningless animal function, bringing a base pleasure only to the male in his dominance over the female. The Women's Liberation Movement in demanding the sexual liberation of women from this dominance, she wrote, would ensure a transition "between simple animal existence and full control of nature."[5] (My mother is particularly offended by this concept that even demeans all animal mating, which she has observed on a farm throughout her lifetime. "You can often see 'love' beyond 'sex' in animals and birds," she claims, recalling her own dogs and horses; remembering the Canada goose that had dropped down out of a great southern-bound formation to spend a desperate winter in a nearby swamp with an ailing mate; and reminding me about both the storks in Belgium that live 70 years and are known to be monogamous and the elephants that live for a century and are strictly monogamous!)

Simone de Beauvoir's condemnation of marriage and motherhood as "the female trap" in her book *The Second Sex*, published in Paris in 1949, was undisguised Marxism, and critics warned that it should be accepted only in its socialist context. At the time editing the Marxist review, *Les Temps Modernes*, with her live-in companion, philosopher Jean-Paul Sartre, she was expounding the socialist philosophy that would equalize men and women into an amorphous mass that could be controlled by the state.

Her thesis she described as "Manichean" — without any gray areas. Men always had all the advantages, had "the good"; women, burdened by their own biology, had nothing but secondary experience, "the bad." She wrote:

> The devaluation of femininity has been a necessary step in human evolution . . . it is male activity that in creating values has made of existence itself a value; this activity has prevailed over the confused forces of life; it has subdued Nature and Woman.
>
> The emancipated woman wants to be active, a taker, and refuses the passivity man means to impose on her. The "modern" woman accepts masculine values; she prides herself on thinking, taking action, working, creating on the same terms as man.[6]

All biological considerations would have to be discarded, she argued, in an "androgynous" world that would be a *brotherhood* (my italics). Women would work to achieve financial independence and autonomy, which would free them from all traditional attachments to men and to marriage and to children. Modern women, she suggested, would avoid marriage — as she had — and avoid children as well.

The Second Sex caused no great stir on this side of the Atlantic when it was first published, but suddenly it was resurrected in the early 1970s by the U.S. Women's Liberation Movement — by then in full bloom — which saw it as another great treatise, an enforcer of feminist ideology. Of course, it too would distance men from women, love from sex, mothers from children.

What kept the author and Jean-Paul Sartre together throughout the years? Was it a mysticism in a "love" she did not understand or was unwilling to acknowledge? Or was it simply accommodation — or nothing more than a determination to live the Marxism she preached? The answer is never clear, despite four autobiographies. Sexually, it seems, the two were incompatible, nor were any of Simone de Beauvoir's numerous sexual liaisons satisfying. Before her death, in a widely quoted interview, she expressed a disillusionment in the doctrines and lifestyle she had advocated. "I abdicated womanhood to become a class collaborationist," she confessed.[7]

Sexual warfare spread into every corner of the English-speaking world with the publication of Germaine Greer's book, *The Female Eunuch*, in which women's role as a sex object required a "passivity" that actually made her a female "eunuch." A stunningly beautiful Australian woman who studied for her doctorate at Cambridge University, she would write — and, later, speak, in a dazzling series of lectures across Europe — with the pseudo-authority of a Cambridge professor: commanding women to cast off "the shackles of marriage, family and sexual repression." She called for nothing less than "the undermining of our civilization" and told her followers "it is time for the demolition to begin."[8]

Demolition in the lives of men and women certainly did begin with the loss of all traditional moral values. Men and women would become polarized in their sexual aspirations, set free for adventure on the "glorious" new sea of promiscuity, where they could forget all about the wonder and mysticism of love to experience earthly "rapture" in the satiation of sex.

Germaine Greer would flaunt her own sexual liberation, and the international press blazoned headlines of her sexual exploits: her posing nude for the pornographic magazine *Suck*; her numerous short-lived relationships, two of them with convicted men of known violence; three abortions; and finally, a disastrous marriage that lasted three weeks.

When Germaine Greer deviated from her original course, many believed the shift was the result of aging and loneliness. She did a near about-face in her later book, *Sex and Destiny: The Politics of Human Fertility*, in which she wrote of "the sterile decadence of western societies" and warned of "the slow suicide of her own culture." In ensuing talk shows in the United States and Canada, she lauded motherhood and children and denounced what she understood as a particularly North American trend toward women's "careerism," which she called a "facet of child-hating." She would repeat, over and over, that "most of the pleasure in the world is still provided by children and not by genital dabbling."[9]

Greer's 1989 book about her father, *Daddy We Hardly Knew You*, may have exposed the roots of an apparent ingrained hatred of men. She stripped him of all dignity and worth, although I would simply judge him as an "ordinary" nonviolent individual, his principal fault being his almost daily withdrawal to his club — a civilized retreat, it would appear, from a shrewish wife and an unloving daughter.

Carolyn G. Heilbrun, who in the 1970s became one of the most prominent leaders in the U.S. Women's Liberation Movement with the publication of her books *Toward a Recognition of Androgyny* and *Reinventing Womanhood*, admired her father extravagantly. Yet she used her mother's life as his wife as the very basis of her major assault on marriage and motherhood. "My mother's terrible failure, as I saw it," she wrote, "helped to make me more feminist than most other women."

Although she produced no evidence, she wrote of her mother's extreme "suffering" — the suffering of "all those mothers whose destinies seemed to their daughters impossibly confined." She elaborated:

> Women have tended not to recognize the pain inherent in lack of selfhood, or if they recognize it to the extent of responding with general depression and despair, they have been unable to articulate it.
> Women's confused response to matrimony, and in her final masochistic acceptance of it . . . must abandon herself. Indeed, if one imagined oneself as newly arrived from Mars and were to read the descriptions of a woman's marriage in contemporary novels by women, one might well ask how on earth anyone could be expected to live out such a farce.[10]

Personally, I have debated with Sheila Copps, a leading Canadian feminist and a 1990 contender for the leadership of the federal Liberal party, this subject of our mothers' destinies, appearing with her on radio and before a packed hall of 700 sometimes cheering nonfeminists. On one radio program, Copps described her own mother's life as "deprived"; yet the life of her mother as the wife (now the widow) of one of the most popular politicians in the Hamilton area of Ontario, as the mother of several remarkable children, as an outstanding contributor to all community affairs, may be seen as a triumph. My own mother's life — her devotion, her nurturing, her musical talents which enrich so many, and her continuing contributions to community — I see as magnificent. Furthermore, I cannot imagine that many career women today are giving more to themselves in the area of self-fulfillment, or are giving more to their country and to the progress of humankind, than our mothers gave.

It is true in Canada that the majority of female politicians are single, dedicated women, or mothers of grown children. Copps is an exceptional feminist role model on the political scene, a Liberal Member of Parliament who gave birth to a daughter at the time the House of Commons was in session. Now a single mother, sharing custody of her daughter with a former spouse, she is able to pay for a trustworthy mother-substitute sitter or nanny.

Of course, denigrating the role and life of the home-keeping mother was absolutely necessary if feminist ideology was to bring about sexual license and the demise of the traditional family. All moral considerations had to be crushed, and mothers, historically, were acknowledged as the chief guardians of our morality. "Old-fashioned" mothers were apt to tell daughters *and* sons:

• Your body is sacred — housing your soul, not to be thrown wantonly away in an open marketplace. (Shakespeare in one of his sonnets claimed that the body's essential purpose was only that of a "mansion" to "house" the soul.)

• Be chaste — would you drink water from the same cup as a dozen transient acquaintances?

• Take the time to find *one* good mate (presumably in courtship), and then have the *guts* — the adaptability, the wisdom, the staying power — to make *marriage* work. Where else but in the solidarity of *family* can you look for any hope of lasting comfort and happiness?

Alvin Toffler, who in his 1971 book *Future Shock* described the former family as the "giant shock absorber" of society, was regretting "the fractured family" and "the limits of adaptability."[11] "Old-fashioned" mothers by the 1980s were seeing happiness becoming so elusive that the word itself was falling into disuse.

Sexual freedom could never bring lasting comfort and happiness into the lives of men and women, yet it was necessary for feminism to promote this lifestyle as an alternative to marriage. Human nature being what it is, with the welling of sexual instincts as predictable as night and day, men and women, once driven apart, would have to be freed from all moral restraints, such as those imposed by monogamy.

Michel Foucault, the internationally renowned French philosopher and social critic, in his three-volume tome *The History of Sexuality* (1978) discussed "desexualization" as a disorientation of all former moral absolutes. Another famous French philosopher and social critic, Roland Barthes, had drawn attention to the "masculinization of women" as observed in the fashion world, in *Sarrasine*, published in 1970.

The masculinization of women was easily discernible across North America as many women aspired to become male clones — not modeling themselves as "gentlemen" (another word fallen into disuse), but as feminists depicted males: macho and oppressive; the predators and the seducers.

Tara Roth Madden in her study *The Uncivil Business* described such women as "ruthless," and a former advertising executive, Edith Gilson, in her book *Unnecessary Choices: The Hidden Life of the Executive Woman*, claimed they lacked "understanding and generosity" in the workplace.[12] This evaluation was apparent when Nadine Winter, a pay equity consultant, brusquely told disadvantaged business leaders at a meeting of the Conference Board of Canada to "stop wringing your hands and muttering . . ."[13] Study after study has confirmed that 90 percent of all men and women in the workforce would prefer to have a male boss.

It seems that men, generally, did not realize they were witnessing the conversion of a minority of women, and so they would hold all women accountable. But even though at the workplace men would walk away from such women, when it came to sexual liberation they accepted the new attitudes that they believed typical of modern feminist women.

Sexual liberation would become a wildly entertaining two-way street of unsatiated lust, unimpeded and encouraged — a sexual permissiveness on a scale never before recorded in any culture in the world. Today, we have been greeted by the disillusionment, the disease and the despair we may have foreseen.

Sex disconnected from love, without any spiritual meaning or commitment, beyond lust, often became simply a sick bodily exercise, many times even lustfully unsatisfying. However, as women espousing feminist ideology were being convinced to ape the feminist writers' macho image of men in the workplace, they were also being led into adopting the feminist image of men in bed.

To gain ultimate equality with men, to have the double standard men had always enjoyed, was seen as the "right" of women, and feminism demanded that any unwanted pregnancies or the children who followed be the responsibility of the state. "Free" abortions and "free" Universal Day Care became top priorities.

Feminist writers deliberately and invariably dwelt on the terrible inequalities of the "double standard." Men had always been promiscuous, they claimed — like the drones they were — flitting from flower to flower. (Of course, there always have been *some* men flitting from flower to flower, seeking and accepting free sex when offered.) The majority of North American men in the years prior to the Women's Liberation Movement may have been "gentlemen," rooted in their parents' and society's moral disciplines, but the feminists would never acknowledge that fact. Nor is it surprising that psychiatric and social studies conducted in the late 1980s indicate that great numbers of young men and a *majority* of young women are willing to admit that they now choose and practice chastity, in expectation of marriage commitments.

The newspaper headline, "Coeds Just as Sexually Active as 15 Years Ago," that appeared in March 1990, was questioned by numerous university students.[14] They wondered if only the most promiscuous students had been the respondents. Some 21 percent of the coeds interviewed for the Brown University survey claimed they already had more than six sexual partners, more than three of them in the year leading up to the survey.

How could such young women still not realize that the abandonment of all moral values, and even of commonsense restraints to random bed-hopping, threatened to result in emotional suffering, in psychic damage, in ruined lives?

A study reported to the American Anthropological Association in 1987 found that in 75 percent of all seductions, women were by then the seducers in society. If you believed the outpouring of feminist articles in all the popular women's magazines, women were also taking over all the initiatives in their sexual encounters, evening an old score and asserting their "right" to equality. Comparing the performance of their various partners became a lively topic for discussion in the consciousness-raising groups and at the luncheon and dinner meetings of the women-only clubs.

Many men, with a far greater sex drive than women, certainly seemed to have enthusiastically welcomed the women's newly struck attitudes toward sex and their learned approaches. How-to books and articles appeared in abundance, and feminists could always turn back to Masters and Johnson for explicit instructions, as well as for reinforcement of their view that sexuality need not be linked to "love" beyond lust.

It was much later that male bewilderment became obvious. The aggressive woman in the workplace, compulsive in her efforts toward equality, in proving that she was as adequate as or better than a man: *that* personality men would be forced to endure, or could avoid, or might be taught to respect. But accepting the Amazonian type of woman in bed? This was another matter altogether.

Then there was the tired-wife syndrome that Ann Landers exposed in a survey that saw 90,000 respondents inform her that they preferred "cuddling" to intercourse. At the same time, psychiatrists and sex therapists were explaining that a satisfying sex life depended on time and energy, and that contemporary women with their frenetic work agendas have little of either at the end of the day.

When rape within marriage became an indictable offense, sexual warfare took a particularly ugly turn. Men and women in the past had found a comfortable accommodation, with wives more often and more willingly submitting to an increased male sex drive. This pattern now could be reversed, with husbands no longer allowed initiation or questionable persuasion. A wife, perhaps newly indoctrinated in a consciousness-raising group or influenced by overwhelming feminist literature into believing in the feminist portrayal of the male, might suddenly imagine a husband's overture as bestial, akin to the vicious crime of rape.

The law could be used as a deadly weapon in dissolving a marriage. If a man were truly innocent, his life would still be in ruins if taken to court on such a charge — a charge as diabolical as a wife accusing an innocent man of child abuse. In both cases a man would find himself powerless and prey to all his wife's demands. And although such instances involving unscrupulous women must be extremely rare, they are publicized and then widely discussed in men's groups, raising a threatening specter in some sexual relationships.

Many men saw themselves as once again immobilized.

First they were denied their competitive drive in a work-place that no longer ensured them of jobs and raises and promotions; these would be *given* by law, unjustly, to millions of women demanding revenge and restitution for a grandfather's supposed discrimination. And now these same men were denied all sexual initiation and consideration. For them, the war of the sexes was over; they were beaten. Was there anything left to do except retreat?

Studies now claim that there are many men who, because they may never again completely trust or respect women, have found that they can expend vast sexual energies in strenuous sports, overcoming sexual appetites. Dr. Beryl Chernick, a well-known London, Ontario, sex therapist, reported in a national magazine that "lack of desire is one of the fastest growing sexual dysfunctions" she was encountering in her practice. "Sexual interest is a very vulnerable part of our systems," she said. "In both men and women, it's related to the brain, not the genitals."[15]

"Signs of Male Alienation on Rise, Conference Told" was the headline of a national newspaper article, June 21, 1989, reporting on an international gathering of 700 mental health experts at the University of Guelph in Ontario, which dealt specifically with sexuality. Dr. Katherine Forrest, a California physician, spoke of the innumerable problems between men and women, often of crisis proportions, and the urgent need to address them:

> An increase in suicides, many cases of sexual dysfunction and even charges of sexual harassment are signs of growing alienation and unhappiness among men . . . Men need understanding . . . While the new male may be a myth, what is not a myth is the distress males are feeling . . .
>
> While women have changed . . . women are demanding more expressive, sensitive men and more skilled lovers . . . they now buy 40 to 60 percent of

condoms for example — they are not free of confusion themselves. Not all are comfortable with the more assertive roles expected of them.[16]

There are 25,000 people who commit suicide in the United States every year, with the peak months — March, April and May — some years indicating an epidemic. Comparative statistics appear in Canada, where the Canadian Association for Suicide Prevention was established as a national emergency measure. In 1989, Statistics Canada reported that 80 percent of the victims were men. All studies suggest that loneliness and isolation are prime causes, with deepening depression a usual forerunner.[17]

Beautiful young women, nonfeminists, certainly not comfortable with the more assertive roles expected of them, are dismayed at a wary expression in the eyes of North American young men they may meet at school or in the workplace.

For example, how very sad that Saturday night is no longer seen as the joyous dating night that used to be expected on any campus. Nevertheless, it has become increasingly evident that more and more young men and young women throughout society have been able to see their way through the clouds — beyond the misconceptions and the confused attitudes and aspirations of our feminist era — to find one another.

Love and sex may indeed blossom *together again* throughout society, growing from understanding and trust and hope.

9

The Alley Cat Syndrome

With sexual liberation, the loosening of all moral constraints accompanied by the denigration of the family, came the prowling: the frenetic searching for casual sex in the one-night stands and the pick-ups; in the personal columns; in the escort services advertisements; in the look-and-choose-a-date video shops; in the singles clubs; and in the relationships with what is known as the two-bit commitment, the kind that can evaporate at a glance.

Infidelity, promiscuity, marriage breakdown and divorce all became a way of life. By the 1970s divorce was rampant. In Canada, the divorce rate rose 500 percent between 1968 and 1983, with a veritable stampede recorded between 1985 and 1987, following the passing of a federal no-fault divorce Act, whereby divorce could be granted after a one-year separation, and a new family law in Ontario that legislated the equal splitting of all assets. In 1989, California, a bellwether of societal mores, was reporting divorces outnumbering marriages.[1]

In an ABC-TV documentary hosted by Peter Jennings,

Betsy Aaron proclaimed that "the age-old idea of virginity is out; divorce is no longer a dirty word; the stay-at-home housewife is becoming part of our history; and instead of one life-long marriage, now it's often a merry-go-round of marriage and divorce."[2]

Marlo Thomas in a *TV Guide* article said she believed women "had grown up," and that this fact was illustrated by comparing the series which she had starred in, in the late 1960s, in which she never slept with her boyfriend, with her series in the 1980s, in which her boyfriend was naturally her lover.

We know now that millions of sexually liberated women left their husbands and homes, having swallowed such feminist ideology hook, line and sinker, only to sink, in disillusionment and despair, their futures bleak. Sadly, once the scales had been lifted from their eyes and they had been made to see those husbands as the oppressive keepers from whom they should shake loose, these women were taught that their biology was a betrayal of "self."

Shulamith Firestone was exhorting women to give up once and for all the traditional "concept of exclusive physical partnerships,"[3] with the suggestion that children then be born to a unit and the blood tie to the mother be ignored. This ideology would surely prove the lowest ebb in the Women's Liberation Movement — separating men from women and women from their own children. The fearful, ultimate result of this thinking became evident when North American society generally began to consider children, the born and the unborn, of little consequence — always of secondary importance. Let other people — the state — care for them when they are young, was the feminist theme. The educational system and television could take over later to teach them about the birds and the bees.

Many parents, blithely abdicating all traditional responsibilities, must have deliberately turned a blind eye to the immense dangers of casting their children — generations of children — adrift from all moral anchors. Leland Goudge of the Toronto Children's Aid Society, Frank Mickens, a prominent New York City principal, and a great many sociologists across North America all have predicted "the loss of generations of children" without a return to moral values.

However, if the alienation of the sexes became most marked among younger men and women, the withdrawal from the sexual liberation of the Women's Liberation Movement has also, in the 1990s, become most significant among this age group. In many studies younger men and women express revulsion at the sexual license of older generations in their promiscuity, their orgies, their infidelities and their divorce. Hardly surprising is the fact that by 1990, divorce had traumatized the lives of half the 18-year-olds on this continent.

Their revulsion may have been sown in the very divorces of their own parents, if infidelity was involved; or in the subsequent promiscuity of a parent. Younger children could be confused, as was the little boy quoted in one study who asked: "Is he my Daddy, or not? Or is the other one my Daddy? I want a Daddy. Jimmy has a Daddy."

While many men and women believed that their sexually liberated lifestyles would be accepted without questioning by their children, we know now that children of all ages have been deeply affected — emotionally and psychologically — and often questioning. Negative reactions in their earlier years, although covert, could in the teen years blossom into extreme hostility toward sexual companions of either parent and then, in adulthood, lead to incurable maladjustment in their own sex lives.

A full-page article in a national newspaper featuring the effect of the AIDS epidemic on "swinging" lifestyles in Canada also discussed the reactions of the children of "swinging" couples. Apparently the majority of parents showed a surprising lack of concern, with one couple quoted as saying that they had "no intention of hiding their philosophy from their seven-year-old daughter." Another couple attempted to keep the details of their lifestyle hidden from three teenagers — surely a remarkable feat. They explained that they had "taken up organized spouse-swapping" with three or four other couples as an alternative to their former separate sex forays outside their marriage. In this case, group sex was established as the rule "after a would-be partner had savaged Gail with his teeth"[4] in a one-couple closed-door encounter.

Ron Michaels, president of Toronto's Club Eros, which has a membership of 676 couples, claims there are as many as 4000 couples in Toronto regularly trading partners in small and large groups. As publisher of an "explicit sex-ad magazine," he is also familiar with two active organized clubs in Edmonton, two in Calgary, one in Windsor, one in Sarnia and as many as five in Vancouver, which is known as the swinging capital as well as the homosexual capital of Canada. Initial contacts for Toronto Eros members usually occur at their Saturday night dances at the Airport Holiday Inn, where "virgins are asked to judge the bubble-gum-blowing contest." In the homes, "a giant hot tub would be advised to provide the 'come-on.'"[5]

At an Alternative Lifestyle convention in Las Vegas attended by members of 250 U.S. and Canadian swing clubs, the main theme attempted to discount the threat of AIDS.

But this is a threat that cannot be discounted, according to many authorities, among them Dr. Pauline Ann Thomas, head of the New York AIDS Tracking Program, which has recorded AIDS as the leading cause of death in New York City among men between the ages of 25 to 44 and women between the ages of 25 to 34. Dr. John Theis, associate professor of psychology and director of family life and sex education studies at the University of Waterloo in Ontario, commented that "members of so-called swinger-clubs may be fooling themselves that honesty is a shield against

AIDS, because spouse-swapping by its nature is a clandestine lifestyle in which information traded is selective."[6]

While consenting adults may surely live as they wish, the fact that some of their children may be influenced to adopt such lifestyles, with AIDS in the offing, is a sobering threat. One defensive swinger did remark: "How can our organized sex be viewed as a greater threat to society than the infidelity known to be prevalent in the rest of the population? It's all cut from the same cloth."

The sexual liberation in the Women's Liberation Movement demanded by leading feminist protagonists such as Germaine Greer, Kate Millett, Shulamith Firestone and Gloria Steinem — who had offered us role models in their own lifestyles — was accomplished when casual sex, with the cold-blooded approach of prostitution, and infidelity became the "norm" in our culture.

Thousands of men and women across North America who have been engaging in sex without love — in raw, unbridled, disease-prone casual sex — will admit that they cannot even remember the names or faces of their innumerable sexual partners. "Sex can be like shaking hands or eating a sandwich, something you do with a stranger when the mood strikes,"[7] one man was quoted as saying in *American Couples*, the book by Dr. Philip Blumstein and Dr. Pepper Schwartz that deals with all aspects of the sexual "coupling" of men and women in North America in the 1980s.

New Woman magazine found 41 percent of the 34,000 married women responding to a 1986 nationwide survey to be having extramarital sex; only 20 percent of the men who responded to the same survey were found to be unfaithful.[8] New Hampshire author Joyce Maynard polled 900 women in her syndicated newspaper column and found 800 of them admit to being unfaithful. Shere Hite was more specific in her book *Women and Love: A Cultural Revolution in Progress*, claiming that her research proved that 70 percent of the women married five years or more were having affairs; moreover, 76 percent of these women insisted they did not experience any guilt feelings. In fact, only 19 percent of all the women in her studies, married, in common-law relationships or single, put their relationships with men first in their lives.[9]

For women's cavalier attitudes and for the worsening of sexual relations between men and women generally, Shere Hite, in all her books, would blame the male. However, because her questionnaires had been mailed out under the letterhead of the New York chapter of the National Organization of Women (NOW), of which she was a member, I would surmise that she used NOW membership lists; thus, the hatred and vindictiveness toward all men in feminist ideology would simply be redesigned into her own theories. Man's patriarchal obstinacy, his lack of skill and sensitivity to a woman's new awareness of her own needs, his refusal to change his sexuality and performance to match hers — all of that was making the sexes incompatible. With divorce a "norm" in society, some women no doubt were persuaded that their husbands were sexually unsatisfying; it was their right to have an affair.

I am convinced that Hite's conclusions were biased beyond belief, the direct result of a tumultuous childhood that saw her suffer the confusion and the pain of three divorces in her family before the age of 14. Her mother's marriages, first to her father, a flight controller, and later to a truck driver, were of a short duration, the latter marriage lasting only two and a half years. Intermittently she lived with her grandparents, who were to divorce after 30 years of marriage, when she would be shipped off to settle with an aunt and uncle in another state. It is surprising to see her today on the talk shows, at 49, clinging to a husband, a German concert pianist 20 years her junior, of whom she speaks in glowing terms.[10]

We know from many studies, including Hite's and those

of government agencies, that women sue for divorce in 75 to 90 percent of all cases (Hite's figure was 90), and that the infidelity of women has become a major factor in marriage breakdown. Many women in the workforce freely admit that they unconsciously compared a "slicked-up" male in the office, or a dynamic operator in the factory, with a sloppy, at-ease spouse in the home setting — the comparisons often leading to extramarital affairs.

The authors of *American Couples* skirted around the expressions — infidelity, cheating, adultery — and simply termed all sex outside a couple's relationship as non-monogamy, a word they decided was inoffensive and morally neutral: "it neither condemns nor condones." Still, they insisted, "the consequences of outside sex . . . whether it occurs by mutual consent or through the purposeful design of one partner . . . cannot but affect the relationship . . . that for many, an act of non-monogamy is the ultimate betrayal."[11]

Although the authors, in their 10-year study, found that 40 percent of the cohabiters engaged in sex outside their relationships, marriage or common-law, the subjects believed that "monogamy is a strongly held moral ideal, even when it is not always adhered to." Furthermore, they had become convinced that "the discipline of fidelity and a measured use of the untruth offer more alternatives for the future than the brutal sincerity of open marriage."[12]

The young men and women of our university population who have grown up in a society that exchanged the "moral ideal" of marriage and monogamy for the sexual liberation offered by Germaine Greer and Gloria Steinem in the Women's Liberation Movement — the soulless promiscuity and infidelity, with all the devastating consequences — have simply been following their elders, but at breakneck speed.

Professor Noni MacDonald of the University of Ottawa reported to the American Society of Microbiology that a survey of 6911 Canadian Students had found 73 percent of the female students and 77 percent of the male students sexually active, many of them admitting to having had 10 sexual partners.[13] A 1987 survey of British university students revealed that the average female student had engaged in sex with six partners. If each of these women's partners was also "average," having had six sexual partners, the study concluded, each "average" female university student has had sexual contact with 43,000 partners.[14]

"They can be pretty 'random' stuff, and 'short-lived,'" one student remarked. "It's better not to let any emotions get out of hand — saves some real agony if you get dumped."

The real agony in abandonment is seen in studies of newly divorced men, who suddenly throw themselves into a promiscuous lifestyle that their friends judge as completely out of character. Such a man may have been celibate before marriage and faithful in marriage, and moreover, he believed his marriage had the strength to endure. However, when his wife departed, taking the children with her (as in 85 percent of the millions of cases), with the explanation that she "needed her own identity," his incomprehension and powerlessness may have demanded instant, if transient, assuaging of his *real agony* in other arms.

Psychiatry Professor Michael Myers of the University of British Columbia, in his book *Men and Divorce*, relates the most serious of mental and physical health problems to the psychological trauma men experience in divorce. He believes that an abandoned husband who suppresses his pain and rage is capable of violence against himself or others; "or more commonly, men will overwork, become substance abusers and fall prey to physical ailments such as migraines, rheumatoid arthritis and coronary disease."[15] Suicide is a recorded result, and Professor Myers suggests that society must pay more attention to the extreme distress of divorced men, must offer more help.

Most psychiatrists agree that, from the cradle to the grave, human beings suffer the greatest real agony in abandonment — a wife's or husband's abandoning a spouse, or a mother's abandoning a child. (Child psychiatrists tell us that in today's society there is nothing a child fears more than the abandonment by one parent in divorce.)

Statistics show that the majority of divorced men remarry within three years, although a significant proportion of these marriages are known to fail; other divorced men will swear off marriage permanently, opting for a less permanent sort of relationship as a substitute. If the men once sought an idealized version of marriage — deep, abiding love and sexual compatibility — the new relationships would still afford companionship, but with a minimum of emotional attachment and no strings attached. They would not be willing to risk any more than that again.

THE RELATIONSHIPS

The risks in marriage could, in one sense, pale in comparison with the risks encountered in relationships, for in a relationship *trust* would always appear to be the missing factor: the trust of one participant in the integrity of the other. Furthermore, if one partner is or becomes more emotionally involved than the other and is abandoned, the pain and injury may be even greater than that of the divorced; in divorce there at least had been an original dream of permanent commitment.

A couple responding to a questionnaire in a study of relationships wrote:

> In this day and age, we are told that there are no sound reasons to believe that marriages can last, so why should we clutter our lives up with all that paraphernalia. So many of our friends whom we consid-

ered to be "in love" and ideally matched, have married and separated within two or three to ten years.
And we've watched them going through divorces that
in some cases crucified them, particularly if there
were kids.

Sometimes we talk about getting married, but I
think we're just plain chicken when it comes to the
decision. And we're not sure we want any children.[16]

A woman responding to the same study explained that
when one partner really does care more than the other, or
has a particularly deep-rooted desire for marriage, he or
she is in a fearfully stressful position, almost "at the mercy"
of the other. The respondent elaborated:

This is so obvious in many relationships, with one
partner aiming to please the other at all costs — never daring to rock the boat — wooing, wooing . . .

I suppose this is how I could describe our relationship. Sid comes from a very conservative family and I
know he never liked this idea of shacking-up. But I'm
only 25, and I have a terrific job, and no intention of
getting married for at least five years. I can see he's
often miserable, and I'm getting tired of a yes-man.
Where would I be without that "open door?"[17]

Lack of fundamental *trust* in each other, in the expectations of any permanence in a relationship, was voiced in a
majority of responses by partners in seemingly compatible
relationships:

I'm just not ready to pin all my hopes on one dame.
Erin's great, and we keep saying "we're in love," but I
would find it hard to trust Erin or any other woman
to keep a promise — as in the marriage ceremony —
to stick to me for life. I guess I've seen too many two-

timing married chicks around the office.

Chuck and I are simply having a "trial run" — who doesn't these days? Of course, we *trust* one another, and have every intention of getting married. But something could happen — one of us could find out something about the other we couldn't stand . . . This is like an insurance policy . . .

This is my fourth relationship, and I'm getting really tired of the variety, comparing, comparing. I keep thinking of what my mother always said — that in a good marriage a couple get to feel like a pair of old shoes, comfortable, usually in step, and always going in the same direction . . . I don't think I ever feel really "comfortable" . . . and it bothers me that in her heart of hearts, my mother considers me a slut . . .

I can't even imagine what kind of man I want anymore, I'm sure I would like to have a kid though, so perhaps this is my chance — to get pregnant and take the baby and run . . . Maybe I'm sick of men . . .[18]

Psychiatrists speak of an emotional sterility — an inescapable cynicism — that develops in men and particularly in women as a result of multiple relationships, a quality also seen in a hastened aging process. The Women's Liberation Movement, determined to free women from all responsibilities in marriage and motherhood, successfully seduced society into accepting the sexual freedom, but at a great price. Leading their "singular" lives, women would be in the greatest danger of losing their capacity to love.

COMFORT IN THE ALTERNATIVES, INCLUDING FEMALE MASTURBATION

As women in the forefront of the feminist movement grew older, and when all women began to find it harder and harder to attract a wary man, alienation of the sexes heightened and feminist writers began to comfort lonely women with fresh new feminist ideology. Hundreds of articles appearing in women's magazines carried titles such as "You Don't Need a Man" and "He's Not Worth the Effort" and "Divorced Women Have All the Advantages." The *Toronto Women's Book* offered a list of such advantages, gleaned from a course that sociologist Lynn Tribbling offered to newly separated women. Some of them were:

Not having to make small talk
Not having to cook when I don't feel like it
Snacking, grazing, eating what I want when I want
Not having to wait for the bathroom
Peace and tranquillity
Financial independence
[Can] turn out the light when I'm ready to
Not being criticized for my personal foibles.[19]

Betty Jane Wylie's *Successfully Single: How to Live Alone and Like It* became a bestselling book. Other books and articles urged women to learn "the skill of solitude." A typical advertisement in *Domino*, a glossy Canadian magazine, featured stunning fashions on a beautiful model who was *playing solitaire.*

Judy Markey, who certainly writes one of the most entertaining syndicated columns in the United States, was the first to describe "the perfect hassle-free bed partner" — a six-foot-long, 20-inch-round down-filled pillow to cuddle up to — "for those of us who have possibly outgrown our teddy bears. Or even more possibly outgrown our wives, our husbands, or our significant others." Advertisements for the "Bed Partner" followed, with prices ranging between $70 and $139.[20]

Another unusual market report indicated that it was becoming popular for women to send flowers to other women. One florist noticed a card accompanying an elaborate bouquet that read: "Congratulations on dumping the bastard, Maisie. He never sent you flowers, anyway."

Judy Markey in another column introduced a contest to find a "trendy name" for her "lost generation — those who are 40-something — pre-geriatric and post-yuppie, and completely different than the 30-somethings angsting around out there." The main differences, she explained, were:

> We don't think we invented babies. Has anyone ever been so tedious about their children? We are also different from the yuppsters because we don't think we invented anguish. And we know for sure we didn't invent sex. In fact most of us can't even remember what sex is . . .
> Our extremely low expectations . . . [don't] exactly mean we're jaded, it's just that we've already dealt with the issues of intimacy, job gratification and quality time. We have discovered that basically, these are concepts that work best in magazine articles.[21]

Jack Todd in a syndicated book review for Southam News marveled at Cynthia Smith's *Why Women Shouldn't Marry*, which suggested there are only two good reasons for a woman to marry: "to collect a man's sperm or his support!"[22]

Still, women must keep in touch with their own sexuality, feminist writers admonished in a flood of articles that introduced female masturbation as the solution. Instructions were explicit.

In *Glamour*, Dr. Penelope Russianoff, author of *When Am I Going to Be Happy — How to Break the Emotional Habits That Make You Miserable*, insisted that it is important for an unattached female to keep thinking of herself as a "sexual being" with "the continuation of sexual activity through self-stimulation and reaching orgasm." The title of her article? "Beat the No-Love-Life Blues."[23]

A *Ladies' Home Journal* article outlined the "how-to" methods for a woman to masturbate that would guarantee an orgasm.[24] Dr. Susan Okie, writing in *Cosmopolitan*, claimed that female masturbation is a "normal activity" and that 95 percent of men and 75 percent of women masturbate at some period during their lives.[25] (These figures are denied in authoritative scientific biological studies.) Prominent Toronto sex therapist Rhonda Katz saw female masturbation as an antidote for stress in a working woman's life. She was quoted in *Health* magazine:

Single women, and many married women too . . . if they are comfortable about masturbation should feel free to indulge in self-pleasuring. This may be especially useful for relieving job-induced stress. Make a date with yourself now and then whether you have a partner or not . . . Light a candle, get into a warm bath, and get rid of your sexual tension by yourself.[26]

There were books of course, such as *The New Our Bodies, Ourselves*, with whole chapters encouraging various practices to ensure that divorce and separation from men need not be the end of a woman's sexual "pleasure."

Shere Hite asserted that the exquisite "pleasure" experienced by a man and a woman in orgasms during intercourse was a myth, and it was undoubtedly this platform that led feminist ideology toward female masturbation. In her bestselling books, *The Hite Report: A Nationwide Study of Female Sexuality* (1976) and *The Hite Report on Male Sexuality* (1981), she argued, indeed, that women do not really enjoy intercourse; that fundamentally it "served only the selfish gratification of the male."[27]

It was surely an unbelievable premise, and one that

could have been accepted only in a feminist era, according to Nicholas Davidson. In his book *The Failure of Feminism*, he explained that Hite's theory, based on pseudo-scientific evidence, was simply another ploy in severing all ties of female dependency on the male. "If men are not necessary for women's sexual fulfillment," Davidson wrote, "then women become free of them."[28]

Masturbation for heterosexual women would naturally bring them closer to lesbian women, who heartily endorsed a heterosexual woman's new no-men lifestyle introduced in feminist ideology. Robin Morgan's *Sisterhood Is Powerful*, an anthology that is actually a vituperative feminist assault on men and former traditional morals and lifestyles, may even have been persuading heterosexual women toward lesbianism. Martha Shelly, in "Notes of a Radical Lesbian," wrote:

> The average man . . . wants a passive sex-object *cum* domestic, *cum* baby nurse to clean up after him while he does all the fun things and bosses her around . . . while he plays either big shot or Che Guevara . . . he is my oppressor and my enemy . . .
>
> Freud founded the myth of penis envy, and men have asked me "But what can two women do together?" as though a penis were the sine qua non of sexual pleasure! Man, we can do without it, and keep it going longer too![29]

Lesbian literature proliferates, particularly in Canada, and full-page newspaper articles celebrate the work of such lesbian writers as Jane Rule, a transplanted American author whose first novel, *The Desire of the Heart*, became a movie, and Nicole Brossard, a Quebec novelist and poet who has won two Governor-General's Awards and explains: "Motherhood made me a feminist. Being in love with another woman made me a lesbian. I feel like I am at the intersection of feminism and lesbianism. The two work together."[30]

California-based folksinger Phranc rates full-page newspaper accounts of her concerts, which often celebrate the homosexual lifestyle. She has said that her ambition is to make "gay" and "lesbian" household words, replacing "faggot" and "dyke."[31]

Gay and lesbian *have* become household words across North America since Kate Millett in 1973 led the feminist forces of NOW against members of the American Psychiatric Association, coercing them into withdrawing their centuries-old diagnosis that designated homosexuality as a "psychiatric disorder." Powerful gay and lesbian journalists, along with politicians such as Sven Robinson, the constantly reelected federal New Democratic Party Member of Parliament from Vancouver and a sponsor of the 1990 Gay Games in that city, have accomplished even more in Canada, where legislation accompanied by substantial government funding (as in numerous grants to theater companies producing plays with homosexual themes) seems to promote the homosexual lifestyle.

HOMOSEXUAL PROMISCUITY AND AIDS

U. S. Chief Justice Warren Burger, in his summation of the verdict in the *Bowers v. Hardwick* case, in June 1986 wrote:

> Proscriptions against sodomy have very "ancient roots." Decisions of individuals relating to homosexual conduct have been subject to state intervention throughout the history of Western civilization. Condemnation of those practices is firmly rooted in Judeo-Christian moral and ethical standards . . . To hold that the act of sodomy is somehow protected as

a fundamental right would be to cast aside millennia of moral teaching.[32]

Such a right, legislated, would "undermine family, marriage and procreation," according to the summation of another case in 1986, whereby the Supreme Court overturned a Georgia Circuit Court ruling to uphold an antisodomy law that was still on the books in 23 other states as well. The media reacted in disbelief in September 1989, when a U.S. immigration officer dusted off an ancient antisodomy law and refused to allow a Canadian to cross the border after he had volunteered the information that he was a homosexual.[33]

There is no doubt that the wide media coverage of the border incident brought back a very painful memory to many Canadians. They had writhed in shame when newspapers across North America had carried accounts of the homosexual activities of a Montreal Air Canada flight steward flying in and out of San Francisco in the early 1980s. During a two-year period, *knowing he had AIDS*, he had admitted to sleeping with 45 different homosexual men in that U.S. city. "Canada's little Hitler," someone called him, "killing off our American cousins."

Phil Donahue, in a September 1989 *Donahue* television show dealing with increasing homophobia throughout North American society, insisted that his panelists acknowledge that homosexual promiscuity had been the major factor in the spread of AIDS. His thesis would become evident in the panelists' various descriptions of the homosexual's lifestyle. One 62-year-old man had consistently sought sexual satisfaction with strangers. "I never cruised the office for partners," he said. "I looked for them elsewhere. And I always preferred bisexual married men."

He may have found them in the parks — the parks in many of the larger North American cities are known to be taken over by homosexual men for their cruising during the summer months — or in the bathhouses, where police raids have proven homosexual men can "connect" with several strangers even in a lunch hour.

In a compassionate article in *Saturday Night* magazine, writer Eileen Whitfield repeated the last words of a dying AIDS victim, Jim St. James, who confessed that "he could have been infected with the AIDS virus by any one of hundreds of men, presumably within a couple of years."[34] Promiscuity is primary in the lifestyles of the majority of homosexual men, according to all studies, and all statistics have established that AIDS infection among North American heterosexuals is minimal in comparison. As well as stemming from the needles in transfusions and those used in drug addiction, AIDS among heterosexuals also has its origins in homosexual practices.

"Privately, many researchers and even some news people acknowledge that they have overplayed the heterosexual AIDS threat," wrote Randy Shilts, a *San Francisco Chronicle* reporter and member of that city's gay community, whose full-time assignment is AIDS coverage for that newspaper. He continued:

> A prominent gay leader, who has long been active in AIDS organization, said: "It was necessary to make them believe they were all going to get it in order to get the government and reporters moving. Unfortunately, the problem will come one of these days when the straights are going to wake up and realize they're not getting it.[35]

Al Neuharth, *USA Today* founder, referring to Shilts in his column "Plain Talk," wondered if this overplaying accounted for the skyrocketing federal and state funds for AIDS research. He pointed out that the National Center for Health Statistics had predicted the number of deaths in 1989 in the United States from AIDS would be 34,388; from cancer, 494,422; and from heart disease, 777,626. "Compare those death totals," Neuharth suggested, "to the federal spending in fiscal 1989 for research and education on each of the three diseases: AIDS: $1.3 billion — Cancer: $1.4 billion — Heart: $1 billion."

The use of condoms for safe sex and the introduction of sex education at the grade-school level were ways to combat AIDS, U.S. Surgeon General C. Everett Koop advised in his *Report on Acquired Immune Deficiency Syndrome (AIDS)*, published in October 1986. However, as a terrified public in the United States and Canada raced to implement both policies, some critics were finding factual errors and omissions in the report that could be responsible for the most serious of consequences. Wayne Lutton in an article in the *National Review* warned: "Koop's so-called strategy for containing AIDS — a combination of sex education for children and the use of condoms — has the potential for causing incalculable harm."[36]

Among the most serious of factual errors in the report was in the statement: "We know that family members living with individuals who have the AIDS virus do not become infected except through sexual contact"; the report also stated that "the AIDS virus has been found in tears and saliva." The British medical journal *The Lancet* in 1984 and 1986 documented cases of the transmission of the AIDS virus within families, where the only known risk factor had been saliva.[37]

The AIDS epidemic has surely struck as much terror among people as did the Black Plague, which ravaged Europe in an earlier era. The hearts of all people must ache for all victims of such a life sentence, and particularly for the children.

CONDOMS VS. MORALS IN THE CLASSROOM

Would those who consider a proposal that condom

vending machines be installed in school washrooms to help in the fight against student pregnancy, AIDS and other sexually transmitted diseases . . . also encourage students to travel in a school bus that has an 83 percent chance of crashing over a five-year period? Of course not. Yet that is the safety record of a cheap condom.[38]

Dr. Richard Gordon, a University of Manitoba biologist, speaking on the Canadian Broadcasting Corporation's *Science Hour* radio program, explained that "a cheap condom with no spermicide has a 70 percent effectiveness over one year in preventing pregnancy, and presumably AIDS. After five years . . . the chance of the uninfected partner becoming infected rises to 83 percent." Other scientists have argued that Dr. Gordon's figures are low: a woman is fertile only for a few days during a month, whereas the AIDS virus may be transmitted any day of the month.

In 1989, the National Institute for Health and the Centers for Disease Control, reporting on a joint research study convened by Surgeon General C. Everett Koop, stated flatly: "Condom use is not a safe practice in preventing AIDS . . . intercourse with a person known to be infected with the AIDS virus is so dangerous anyone in such a situation should consider alternative methods of expressing physical intimacy." The virus has a diameter smaller than the pores of the latex and it may flow through, and there are other risks, such as unseen defects, breakage, slip-off and spillover.[39]

Health authorities across the continent have been deeply concerned that the present public concentration on the AIDS crisis together with the promotion of the universal use of condoms for all safe sex has been lulling the public into believing that condoms can also slow down the increasing incidence and ravages of other venereal diseases.

In the spring of 1989 the Centers for Disease Control estimated that there would be 7.5 million new cases of the five most common sexually transmitted diseases before the end of that year: chlamydia, gonorrhea, syphilis, genital warts and herpes. Chlamydia causes 50,000 women each year in the United States to become infertile. In 36 percent of the women and 13 percent of the men with primary genital herpes, meningitis develops; the onset of that disease is recognized by fever, headache, vomiting and rigidity in the back of the neck, and it often leads to death.[40]

It has also been estimated that between 10 and 20 percent of the women in North America between the ages of 18 and 35 are infected with HPV, the deadly human papilloma virus. It is now known to appear in 50 or more subtypes, and is associated in 90 percent of the cases of cervical intraepithelial neoplasis (CIN). Thousands of women throughout North America each year die from cervical cancer. The fearful aspect of HPV is that there are no early symptoms.[41]

"This is something that will kill far more Canadian women than AIDS," Dr. Michael Shier, chief of obstetrics and gynecology at Toronto's Wellesley Hospital, told Kristin Jenkins in an interview reported in the September 1989 issue of *Flare* magazine. By the end of that year, Dr. Shier estimated, the Wellesley Hospital alone would have treated 5000 women in its CIN clinic. Dr. Alex Ferenczy, gynecologist and pathologist at Montreal's Jewish General Hospital, insists that the sexual partners of any woman with CIN be tested for the human papilloma virus.

In 1986, according to a *Time* magazine poll, 86 percent of the parents in the United States had voted for increased sex education in the schools, which could include graphic sex instruction of heterosexual as well as homosexual practices — beginning at the third-grade level. Dr. Harvey Fineberg, dean of the Harvard School of Public Health, had told parents: "We are at a point where sex education is no longer a matter of morals — it's a matter of life and death."[42]

I believe the majority of parents across North America must have realized the appalling danger of deliberately choosing to replace moral teachings with condoms and sex education. There were certainly many teachers throughout the systems who warned of the consequences, seeing an intensified preoccupation with sex leading to a fresh burst of promiscuity among adolescents. The concerns of these teachers would be continually overruled in the media and in legislation.

By 1989, a pattern of increased promiscuity had become evident. The number of teenage pregnancies had risen dramatically, and statistics began to record both the growing number of teenage deaths from AIDS and increases in all other sexually transmitted diseases among adolescents.[43]

"Can we stem the tide?" asked one teacher in an Ontario study. He wrote:

> For ten years, at least, we have been telling the kids that sex is natural, openly and insidiously suggesting that its expression should not be repressed. In the last four or five years we have been giving them the most graphic, "how-to" instructions — relying on condoms, of course.
>
> We've told them, "It is your body and it is your decision — when and whether to engage in sex . . ." Didn't we realize that this was pretty "heady" stuff for 13, 14, 15-year-olds — to be told that he or she alone had the "right" to make such a momentous decision?
>
> In a traditional era, in an almost forgotten world, teenagers had always been relying, comfortably, on others to make that decision — their parents, their teachers, the churches — society generally. If one kid fell by the wayside, well, there was always that

straight road out there somewhere, and one could get back on to it.

Where is the straight road today? We've been handing our kids raw sex, undiluted, the most powerful force in human nature — without even a smattering of moral deterrent. Is it not time for society, the churches, teachers and parents, particularly, to stop pussy-footing around with our teenagers and start building some straight roads and some *fences*.

Never mind that we, ourselves, have been sexually liberated, offering them role models in the promiscuous lifestyles that — we might now point out to them — have brought many of us to the miserable *end* of our road. We could still have a try at saving our civilization through our kids.[44]

This whole picture became clear when 1989 studies of the transmission of the AIDS virus indicated that the alarming numbers of young men and women in their early 20s acquiring the disease may have been infected during their teen years. The university population would come under particular scrutiny.

The first major achievement of the Women's Liberation Movement was the desegregation of campus residences across North America. There had been widespread resistance among undergraduate men and women who believed a one-sex dormitory provided a relaxed climate, certainly more attuned to intensive study, but their objections fell on deaf ears. Doggerel turning up in one of the university weeklies at the time ended: "temptation stalks the halls — bare feet, bare bodies in our shower stalls."

When campus rape became a frightening aspect of university life, the governors of Alberta's University of Lethbridge in 1989 decided once again to segregate the sexes in their campus residences. Although the news was greeted by cynical amusement in newspapers across the continent, in university circles there is a suggestion of a trend — if feminist laws will allow it to happen.[45]

Many administrators see a dual purpose being served: defusing the extreme hostility between male and female students that happens in the close quarters in some of those coed residences, and restoring some of the traditional values found in former university lifestyles. One professor, 46 years old, happily married and definitely not out of touch, remarked: "Let them stand back from one another — and then come together with some of that 'old-fashioned' courtesy and respect for one another that we've all forgotten about. Instant intimacy is for the birds — and that's not true either; if you're a birdwatcher you'll know that every species has a courtship ritual."

Perhaps it is on the campuses of North America that we must begin to find the tools to heal society. Perhaps there we will see the armistice that will end the war of the sexes of the past three decades — the war instigated and still fueled daily by radical feminists in the Women's Liberation Movement; the war that grew uglier and uglier in the 1980s.

A whole new program can be introduced, concentrating on both *bringing men and women together again* and *bringing love and sex together again*. Women in the women's studies programs may even be persuaded to cross over: to leave those man-hating courses behind them, to rejoin the mainstream of society, to communicate again with the opposite sex. We know that as long as they remain in those programs, they will have little opportunity to communicate with the opposite sex. Numerous surveys have proven that *men simply do not date the women attending those women's studies classes.*

Men and women have always realized that history is the most important subject in preparing for the future. Our lives may be meaningless if we are trapped in a minuscule time zone: not learning from our past, not having the deepest concern for our future — the future of our children and of our civilization. So many men and women have already learned the hardest history lessons from their own immediate past, from surviving extreme suffering — the derangement in their own lives; the divorce; and, often, the promiscuity of their parents. They have learned as they struggled past peers drowning in early sex and past schoolmates who were victims of the drug culture. (All of this decadence relates to the portrayal of amorality in Denys Arcand's internationally award-winning play and film, *The Decline of the American Empire*.)

Older, haggard women — denaturalized, masculinized (in Roland Barthes' opinion) and sexually spent — and disillusioned men (desexualized, according to Michel Foucault) may be unable to break loose from a feminist society's sexual norms of the 1970s and '80s — even under the terrifying pall of the AIDS epidemic. Yet our young men and women in the '90s may be able to muster the strength and discipline to leave sexual liberation behind them — back in their parents' era — and to redesign and rebuild a happier, safer society.

It seems that even chastity (another old-fashioned term denied in past decades) can become a "norm" — or at least one that is aspired to — in their era. Internationally known Freudian scholar Helen Puner wrote a book about chastity. It cannot be found on the shelves in the women's studies departments, but male and female students are reading it. The book, written as a letter to her own daughter, is entitled *Not While You're a Freshman*. Helen Puner writes:

I'll try to take first things first. First is this: For girls and women like you — the organic kind, not the plastic dolly kind — sex isn't just a coin and slot-machine affair, a stripped down lab question of stimulus and response. It's a lot more. The fact that for a woman, sex is taken internally, is a basic clue to its feminine nature. Sexual response for a woman comes from the inside — and goes out. It doesn't come from the outside and go in. (I'm talking about *response*, not stimulus.) Since it's taken internally, you have to have something tuneful inside with which to set the words to music.

For a girl, sex engaged in because a revolution's being fought and it's *your* revolution; or because you're afraid of not having dates, or of losing a boy; or because it's "good" for you — is a long way from this state of attunedness . . . Without the tune, sex for a woman isn't terribly important — and indeed, may be downright ludicrous or unpleasant. May be a great big flop or a tiny dull thud — instead of the joy, the root enhancer and replenisher of life it also can be . . . Sex has a context, Laura — and it can be good or bad depending on what you bring to it . . .

All right, I *know* your generation has been told to quit fussing — that too much fuss has been made over a simple instinctual act. That it needn't and shouldn't be overlaid with deposits of emotional investment, with societal traps like marriage, and many more reasonable arguments of that nature . . . Take it easy, take it cool . . . sex is a biological drive no more earthshaking than any other.

. . . And yet, and yet, I get the feeling that you people also hanker for the exact opposite — that the earth shakes a la Hemingway when good bedfellows get together . . . so formidably romantic that Byron might be all shook up?[46]

PART
III

*Mothers
and
Children*

When Eve was brought to Adam he became filled with the
Holy Spirit, and gave her the most sanctified, the most glorious of appellations, he called her Eva, that is to say, *the
mother of all.* He did not style her wife, but simply mother
— mother of all living creatures. In this consists the glory
and the most precious ornament of woman.
Martin Luther, 1517

The future of society is in the hands of the mothers. If the
world was lost through woman, she alone can save it.
Louis de Beaufort, 1795

10

Golde, Do You Love Me?

In my favorite of classic musicals, *Fiddler on the Roof,* Tevye demands to know if Golde "loves" him after 25 years of marriage — an arranged marriage. Golde, analyzing her feelings in song, finally supposes that she does. Tevye supposes he loves her, too, and that after 25 years "it's nice to know." Their love would have been cultivated in traditional commitment, to flourish as they shared all the tribulations of an oppressed people in a small Russian village and all the joys and comfort of their religious beliefs and parenthood. Their love would be reflected in the true-love matches of three daughters.

In an interview, Pat and William Buckley, married 40 years and claiming they had never known "a moment's doubt about the rightness of their union," were asked, "What makes your marriage work?" Pat mused, "Maybe we just like each other." He credited "the psychic consummation in marriage."[1]

Albert Camus in his novel *The Plague* wrote:

A loveless world is a dead world, and always there comes an hour when one is weary of prisons, of one's work and of devotion to duty, and all one craves for is a loved face, the warmth and wonder of a loving heart.[2]

Perhaps love must always be cultivated in commitment in marriage. Like a plant, it can be difficult to nurture, but there is the promise of lifelong bloom. Perhaps the health of our society, generally, will begin an upturn, will stabilize, if men and women throughout the Western world again believe in lifetime commitment in marriage and not in the expectation of divorce. We do know that many men and women today will marry only after planning a legally satisfying divorce in the signing of their marriage contracts.

The vast differences in the very natures of men and women, differences that feminism so radically denies, must present the greatest challenges in the earliest and shakiest years of marriage, when the majority of unions falter. In the earliest years, dreams and hopes may always dim, as each partner in intimacy comes to recognize the failings and weaknesses in the other — the failings and weaknesses that exist in every other human being on earth.

The simple belief in a lifetime commitment in marriage may be enough to head off the swift and hurtful reactions to crises in the earliest years of marriage. You learn to curb your tongue, the most deadly of weapons in all human relationships; and you find that there is *time* to seek understanding and adjustments and compromise. Even miracles can happen when partners remember their promise of *time*. The stakes are incredibly high.

Maggie Scarfe, author of the bestselling *Intimate Partners*, in an interview reported in *Time* agreed that "anybody who has been married for longer than 15 minutes knows that there are problems." In her studies, reported in her book, she saw a lessening of the tension between men and women, a refusal to accept Shere Hite's "picture of a pervasive and profound despair in the alienation of the sexes." Scarfe writes:

> Falling in love has to do with summoning up inchoate, rapturous feelings of engulfment in a safe and intimate world — one in which two are as one, perfect company, and in which perfect nurturance exists. It has to do with the visions of Eden, buried within, before human aloneness had been perceived.[3]

We cannot doubt that men and women belong together on this earth, that they are incomplete without one another, in mind and soul and body. Nor can we question that the institution of marriage, the *sanctified* spiritual-physical union of men and women, has proven an ideal institution in the evolution of civilization. In the building of nations and the growth of humanity, marriage and the traditional family have long been acknowledged as the principal sources of great strengths. They are, after all, based on the "nurturance" of the spirit, as well as the "nurturance" of all physical needs.

Men and women have throughout the ages thrived on their interdependence in marriage, leaning on one another, supporting one another. It was that very interdependence that feminism could not countenance. Betty Friedan in an epilogue to *The Feminine Mystique* had set the course, directing

> a sex-role revolution for men and women which will restructure all our institutions: child rearing, education, marriage, the family, the architecture of the home, the practice of medicine, work, politics, the economy, religion, psychological theory, human sexuality, morality, and the very evolution of the race.[4]

Muriel Dimen, in *Surviving Sexual Contradictions*, suggested "a world without gender, where sexual events occur between individuals of any persuasion and eroticism infuses everyday life with pleasure."[5] What she simply failed to understand, however, is that we *cannot* survive — and that we *are not* surviving — all our sexual contradictions. Men and women wantonly choosing unbridled promiscuity in our feminist era may have reached a sterility of mind and soul and body. We have experienced the "bitter tastelessness of shadow fruit," in T. S. Eliot's words.[6]

Poor, demented Sylvia Plath, who finally committed suicide. She became a famous feminist heroine by describing her sexual experimentation, in her novel *The Bell Jar*, but she illustrates ultimate disillusionment in feminist ideology's sexual liberation. Sophocles, the greatest Greek dramatist, explained in his drama, *Ajax*:

> When reason's day sets rayless, quenched, joyless in
>   cold decay,
> Better to die and sleep the never-waking sleep,
> Than linger on and dare to live,
> When the soul's life is gone.

I believe Plath and innumerable other women, as well as men, may lose their souls in promiscuous lifestyles.[7]

Of course, there are those who deny that we have a soul. But, as my mother has always said, "Can anyone on earth tell us truthfully that they believe we are nothing but a hank of hair and a bunch of old bones?" One senses the yearning for change, the wish to lift ourselves up again to higher ground. Perhaps we can regain our souls in more ordered, morally disciplined lifestyles, in which we can again expect the happiness that has proven so elusive to so many during the past decades. Happiness: the word itself was lost in the worsening relationships between men and women.

DO WE SEE A NEW DAY DAWNING?

Life magazine, with 38 pages of new-old love stories in its April 1990 issue, focused on new attitudes toward love and sex, but often with old themes. One article heralded the return of Johnny Mathis, who was rekindling romance with all his old prefeminism songs — "Wonderful, Wonderful," for example, which had broken all records by staying on the charts for nine years. A new generation is singing along: "Walk my way . . . and a thousand violins begin to play."

"I always think of romance as walking on the seashore by the sand dunes," Mathis is quoted as saying. "I see purity, real purity, not decadence. The sand dunes and sea air, Patti Page, old Cape Cod, the broken fences and two people walking along holding hands . . ."

There was only one dismal note, in another article in the magazine. "Before a love affair can begin," the article pointed out, "people have to meet — and nowadays that's easier said than done . . . With 66 million men and women [in the United States] single and eager to mingle, there's a gasping need here."

However, I believe that when men and women begin to understand one another again, begin to trust one another again, and begin to face these problems, *together again*, "mingling" will come naturally. They will find one another not in the "cozy booths installed in launderettes" or the video agencies, or the singles clubs, but at former match-making haunts: the churches, the colleges and universities, the workplace and the Sunday suppers that used to be a tradition with the rich and poor.

Perhaps in the phenomenal success of a brand new pop-rock group, the New Kids on the Block, we *are* seeing a new day dawning. The songs of these dynamic teenagers, such as "I'll be Loving You Forever," "Please Don't Go, Girl," and "This One's for the Children," have been on top of the charts in the United States, Canada and

Britain. Their album *Hanging Tough* soared to the top of the British charts, and their 10-day tour through England proved a record sellout, with the critics estimating that their popularity exceeded that of the Beatles in their heyday. In the United states 7.6 million copies of *Hanging Tough* were sold before March 1990.

Teenagers will wait two or three days in all weather conditions, under all circumstances, to buy tickets to New Kids concerts. Teenagers — *who are our future* — are listening to them, loving them, following them. The group receives 30,000 fan letters every day, such as the one that promised: "I will never drink or take drugs because you think it's bad." One of their fan phone lines carries the message, "Say no to drugs."[8]

If Boston became notorious as a city of drugs and criminals, it is beginning to shine again as the home of the New Kids on the Block, especially because of their influence in the "Stop Drugs" campaign. Former Massachusetts Governor Michael Dukakis rewarded the boys for their antidrug work by designating April 24 New Kids on the Block Day, one of the city's highest honors. At the Boston Music Awards the group received two awards for "You've Got It — The Right Stuff," one for best single of the year, the other for the video of the song. The prestigious American Music Awards in 1989 voted *Hanging Tough* best album and New Kids on the Block top pop-rock band.[9]

Thousands of articles and books tell the teenagers all about the family-oriented lives of their idols. Jon and Jordan call their "mum" nearly every time they reach a new town, and the calls often last an hour. When all their "mums" gather to hear them, the boys call them the "Posse 30" (the "mums" have 30 kids among them). When they finish their exhausting tours, the boys can't wait to get back to their old neighborhoods. Joey still attends Catholic high school and this year was an altar boy at the wedding of his drama teacher. While they work doggedly under an inspired record producer, Maurice Starr, whom they consider an "older brother" as well as their founder and manager, they credit their success to their religious roots.

Robin McGibbon, who writes for two London newspapers and is a New Kids biographer, explains:

> Before each show, the New Kids and Maurice Starr go through a two-minute ritual no one would ever dare interrupt. They huddle up in a tight circle in the dressing room, or behind the stage, and pray. They close their eyes and hold each other's hands and one of the boys, or Maurice, says a prayer to thank God for their musical talent, and to bless each other and their families and the ones they love . . . It was eithe-Donnie's or Maurice's idea and it began when they played their first gig at the Lee High School . . .[10]

Donnie, who is the best rap artist and breakdancer ever to shake loose the footlights, has even more ideas, which are just as astonishing to a jaded society satiated in loveless and dangerous sex, such as "Hanging Tough" and "I'll Be Loving You Forever." But he and Danny and Joey and Jon and Jordan have captured the young; and, of course, the young have the future of our world in their hands.

I suppose we may consider the New Kids on the Block to be harbingers of a new and brighter era, in which even little children may be given back a two-minute prayer time at school. In this new age, men and women will seek one another, and they will find the "true" love the poets have promised, the spiritual crowning of passion, with love and sex back *together again.*

11

Motherhood

Motherhood is selfless devotion, unquestioning love and an open door to the eternal. There is no other role that offers the joys, the challenges, the responsibilities and the potential power to influence and shape society. Abraham Lincoln said it all in acknowledging: "All that I am or hope to be, I owe to my angel mother."

Motherhood is the Virgin Mary cradling the Baby Jesus in her arms in the very greatest art the world has ever produced. It is Teresa Smith, who in 1989 underwent surgery to give her ailing baby daughter, Alyssa, part of her own liver — and the wondrous gift of life a second time. It is the mother in Ethiopia, still pouring boundless love and comfort from her own wasted body into that of her starving, dying child as she presses him close to her. And it is the thousands of mothers today who are bringing motherhood back from a veritable wasteland.

Is there anyone who can deny that motherhood has become a veritable wasteland, particularly in North America, where feminist ideology successfully established the single cult and motherhood-on-the-run as the "norm"? Germaine Greer told an interviewer that we had developed a "child-hating culture in North America." So, why not let state day care, the schools, the television, nurture our kids? "We simply haven't the time. We have so many better things to do."

With the feminist denaturalization of women, society generally came to be persuaded that the truly "good life" for many women did not necessarily need to include children. The absolute freedom from such onerous responsibilities, the pursuit of their own singular aims and pleasures, could outweigh the exquisite joys and the unlimited rewards of unselfish parenthood. Many women, not necessarily lesbians, would decide to live apart from men, choosing the ultimately free-and-easy, no-responsibility lifestyle.

There were other women, seemingly determined to defeat life, who would rely on abortions, with one in three fetuses aborted in the United States and a higher percentage estimated in Canada, where the Supreme Court struck down all deterrents. How many prime ministers and presidents have been lost in these decisions? In demographic circles on both sides of the border, there is certainly panic at our plunging birthrates. In Canada, with the second-fastest falling birthrate in the world (after Japan), the Department of Health and Welfare published a study in 1989, explaining the extremely serious economic implications in a top-heavy aging population. The report, *Charting Canada's Future*, urged massive immigration, without which "continuation of Canada's below-replacement rates would eventually lead to Canada's disappearance."[1]

The most serious threat to the unique character of Canada, of course, is in the gradual loss of the French language. The Quebec government in 1988 had declared a crisis, and it now offers tax incentives, subsidies and other benefits to mothers giving birth to three or more children.

At the same time, the province must plead for French-speaking immigrants from Europe and Asia and Africa, who may bring strong traditions of family life with them.

The most devastating accomplishment of the Women's Liberation Movement on this continent has been the near-demise of the family, with women induced into leaving their homes and their husbands and, saddest of all, their children behind them.

Betty Friedan had actually been able to convince many women that "they had better things to do," that "motherhood, wifehood, sexual love, family responsibility" had no right to "use up, to dispose of women's creative energies." One day it will seem incredible that so many had accepted her views, founded as they may have been on her own failures and frustrations. She had written:

> Perhaps it is only a sick or immature society that chooses to make women "housewives," not people. Perhaps it is only sick or immature men and women, unwilling to face the great challenges of society, who can retreat for long, without unbearable distress, into that thing-ridden house and make it the end of life itself . . . at work an eight-year-old could do — peculiarly suited to the capacities of feeble-minded girls.[2]

The logic was ludicrous, ignoring history, ignoring the strengths and achievements of North Americans that were based on the traditional family structure. The stability, security and happiness found in the family lifestyle, the family team, had been responsible for building the greatest society on earth, with women's creative energies expended in the grandest, most important, and most rewarding work of all.

(The househusbands of modern times, at home caring for children, must be interested to know that Friedan considers such an occupation "peculiarly suited to the capacities of feeble-minded girls." Day care workers across the land, so many of them now entrusted with the most important work in the world, must also be interested to know how feminist ideology ranks their work.)

There were those women who would follow Friedan, and then one another, blindly. (As blindly as my father's sheep, it seems, who follow one another from pasture to pasture, driven by a little black-and-white sheepdog and never raising their heads, never veering off the narrow path.) Certainly, there have always been those cop-outs who compare the incredibly strenuous physical, mental and emotional demands of motherhood with the slicked-up and far easier demands of the workplace and "opt" for a *one-dimensional* job. If conscience ever bothered them, there was always feminist reinforcement in all media to assure them that "all women *must* work now for economic survival" — another feminist lie.

So many of the think tanks on the continent along with magazines such as *Fortune* have pointed out that fewer than 30 percent of the women in North America *must* work for economic reasons — that middle-class women have always been able to *choose* the traditional family lifestyle, a right denied in feminist ideology. This is a right that radical feminist leaders today fight to take away through the taxing of sole-supporting husband-fathers to pay for day care they do not wish or need, ultimately leading to the socialist objective of Universal Day Care.

In a 1990 study, one young mother, who had resigned as a department store manager when she gave birth to her first child, claimed it was simply a matter of "lowering one's expectations." She explained that she had "learned to clean her own clothes"; as they were all perfectly good, they would be lasting her a long time. She had learned to cook inexpensive meals that were probably a lot better than the frozen, prepared fast-food purchased before. Jake, her husband, had picked up and fixed a lot of furniture that people had put out for garbage. They no longer went to the movies, but found a great selection of free films to borrow from the local library. Their small rented house was 20 miles out of town, but they had been able to sell their second car, with Jake usually commuting by train. And there were new friends, other stay-at-home mothers in the neighborhood, all swapping kids' clothes and equipment.

"It had to be a joint decision — that I would stay home," the young mother explained, "but I think it might have also saved a shaky marriage. I believe Jake and I are more 'in love' now than we were before we were married. I figured out that we simply have a lot more time now in our lives for all the little kindnesses, for all the little things we do for one another without being asked. And of course, we adore the kids, and are determined they are not going to grow up like a lot of those poor mixed-up kids we read about in the papers every day."[3]

Never having enough time to spend with one's children is often an agonizing plight of mothers in the workforce. Of course, in our feminist era, the media continually offer remedial guidelines. Such as: "Give your child one hour of quality time a day" (a social service message appearing on Canadian television screens throughout 1988). Or, from family therapist Kathleen Tribe, speaking to a *Toronto Star* conference for working parents:

Take the first 12 minutes in the house doing nothing — nothing — but relaxing with the children . . .

Don't open the mail while chatting about school. Don't feed the cat. Don't flip through the paper.

Take 12 minutes — a number deliberately too specific to just guess at — to play, to read a story, just talk.

A "frazzled" young mother, reporting on that conference, wrote:

> Gosh, a whole 12 minutes with my child? But at the end of the day, with work still on your mind, traffic on your nerves, guilt at leaving your kids still in your heart and nothing in your stomach, many of us need some pretty basic tips.[4]

That "frazzled" young mother needed help, certainly, but the conference didn't even mention what one hour, or that 12 minutes, could do for the child. Even cats or dogs may not thrive with so little attention.

Women business executives as well as men take their work home with them, and, according to a Priority Management Systems survey of executives in North America, Britain, Australia and New Zealand, average less than two hours a week looking after their children. Sixty percent of those polled earned more than $40,000 a year; 89 percent admitted taking work home, and 65 percent said they worked at least one weekend every month; 48 percent experience daily stress, including severe headaches and stomach problems.[5]

"Executive Kids: The Neglected Generation" was the sadly appropriate title of an article reporting a study by Jon Ferry for Reuters. Although this study failed to deal with the severe psychic problems of mothers in the executive suite, other psychiatric studies have shown that the majority of mothers in the workforce, if they have jobs involving any real responsibility, cannot detach their minds from the large and small problems of the day when they open the front door to greet their children. Nor are they able to turn off all their large and small worries concerning their children the moment they punch in at the office or the factory in the morning. It seems their psychic suffering often results in disorientation and, in extreme cases, mental breakdowns. Accelerated aging also seems to result.

"It's really devastating what's happening," Kathie Tait, a Vancouver family relations counselor, was quoted as saying in her assessment of the greater damage to children in our current lifestyles. "Children are a very low priority in our society," she claimed. "We are seeing the effects of this already, and it's going to get worse."[6]

There will always be unusually talented or skilled workforce wondermothers who seem to "have it all": successful marriages, and children (the majority of them brought up by superior mother-substitutes) who exhibit little indication of any deprivation. And there are the mothers, particularly single mothers, who truly must work and need society's full support in raising their children. But the majority of women on this continent are known to be middle-class, *and they must have the right to choose their own lifestyles.*

Simone de Beauvoir, in an internationally reported discussion with Betty Friedan in 1975, stated flatly: "Women should not have that choice, precisely because if there is such a choice, too many women will choose to be a homemother."[7]

The ultimate legislation that feminists fight for throughout the United States and Canada would be as ironclad as that in socialist Sweden: regimenting all women arbitrarily out of their homes into the workplace, and all their children out of their homes into state day care, with all democratic rights forbidden. Already in North America a woman's *right* to make her own choice of lifestyle is being surreptitiously whittled away by the unfair taxing of sole-supporting fathers and the state funding of lower and lower grades in the elementary school system.

We must hope that the majority of women across North America will soon turn their backs on Betty Friedan and Simone de Beauvoir and fight to regain their lost ground and their unqualified *right of choice*, and then demand that society respect their choice.

If more and more mothers across North America *choose* to take their great assortment of talents and skills back home again, to care for husbands, to raise their own children in a moral, ordered, stable, secure environment — joining the mothers already at home — our families may be restored to their traditional strength and influence. It is encouraging that 59 percent of the women of North America have been keeping the home fires burning, holding firm to our roots and probably ensuring our future.

At a convention in Lethbridge, Alberta, of the Alberta Federation of Women United for Families (AFWUF), hundreds of women reported on small businesses they had established at home in order to earn extra money and bridge the transition from workplace to home. One at-home mother, an accountant, spends a few hours a week looking after the books of her dentist-husband and his associate. One mother of three teenage girls spoke of a happy family involvement in pottery, with brisk sales. Innumerable other crafts, some learned from grandmothers, are reappearing as small home industries that generate great interest among all family members. How-to workshops at the convention were accompanied by a master list of 89 suggestions for small at-home enterprises reflecting every level of skill.

At that same convention, farm mothers spoke of the joys and incredible closeness of parents and children in farm families, with all members sharing in interests, chores and decisions. Mothers who are partners with their husbands in stores told of a similar solidarity in their families. Many women said that for them part-time work was the answer; nurses, for example, spoke of enjoying their one- or two-night shifts each week or month. Current studies indicate that more and more mothers across North America are retreating to part-time work outside the home, with many of these women ultimately deciding to become full-time homemakers. Meanwhile, economists across North America have been predicting that men and women, by lowering their expectations and slowing down the overspending rampant in past decades, may have considerable impact in improving the domestic economy.

Those women who packed the meetings at the AFWUF convention offered hundreds of ideas on how to strengthen the family and save the family. Always, one message was clear: Get your priorities straight.

Attending that convention, where I addressed and learned from that enthusiastic crowd, I was particularly able to relate to that message. I had left a successful career in journalism, as an editor of national magazines and an interviewer on national radio, to become a full-time homemaker who nurtured a husband and children and had time and energy for relatives and community. I faced the exciting challenges and experienced the joys, the rewards and the self-satisfaction which are part of the traditional family lifestyle that feminist ideology has so denigrated.

A mother at home, loving a loving husband, accepting the joint responsibility of raising their children, may still have her physical and psychic capabilities taxed beyond imagination, resulting in her growth. In my own case, I certainly grew with my children and also through my volunteer work with the IODE, a Canadian women's organization in which I became a national officer. All members, helping to establish pioneer villages, became amateur historians; and, in the building and support of community centers and nursing stations throughout the far north, we became experts in Arctic affairs. There are boundless opportunities for personal growth and enrichment when a woman chooses homemaking with a husband and children as her career. Caring for one's family has invariably extended into volunteer service.

Of course, homemothers have always been the backbone of volunteer organizations, and there is no doubt that society has suffered generally with the withdrawal of their services during our feminist era. The infamous 1971 resolu-

tion by the National Organization of Women (NOW) in the
United States, urging women to volunteer for social change
in feminist groups but *not* for community service, where
their labor would be exploited, was repudiated by Betty
Friedan herself in her 1981 book, *The Second Stage.*[8]

Reuniting mothers and children will save our families
and may be absolutely imperative in restoring security and
stability and happiness to the lives of our children. There
are very few women in the 1990s who will not admit that
motherhood-on-the-run has been a shabby substitute for
the real thing, denying a woman her inalienable role of
caring for her own children.

12

Childless, Lesbian Socialist Leaders in the Women's Liberation Movement

Childless feminist leaders have pried our precious children out of our arms. As we have left our children screaming in day care, our own hearts breaking, feminist leaders have reassured us that we are not truly fit to raise them ourselves, that other women are more qualified — some of them very wonderful women, but considered of the very lowest worth according to wage scales. Socialist feminist leaders, determined that every area of our lives be controlled by the state, have separated us permanently from our children — forcing us, under feminist ideology, to languish throughout all our days in one-dimensional jobs in the workplace. Meanwhile, so many of our teenagers drown in drugs and sex in empty afternoon houses — the houses that no longer deserve to be called "homes," for sometimes they are so lacking in moral supports and selfless loving.

How could we women — how could North American society, generally — have allowed the feminist revolution to succeed? There is no doubt that the majority of women across North America who read Betty Friedan's *The Feminine Mystique* in the 1960s initially dismissed it as simply the caterwauling of an unhappy, frustrated wife and mother — a square peg in a round hole. Since then, of course, we have all found Friedan to be a moderate. By the 1980s she was seen as retreating from many of her 1963 admonishments: desperately trying to replace traditional families with new concepts, such as communal-type groupings, which, she has admitted, consistently fail; and condemning the fearful alienation of the sexes and the neglect of children (which, I believe, have certainly resulted from the Women's Liberation Movement).[1]

Friedan had launched the Women's Liberation Movement, but it was the powerful feminist leaders who followed her — childless, lesbian and socialist — who could claim responsibility for the successes of a social revolution that would change society throughout the Western world. Its most heartless aspect, with the most far-reaching consequences, would be the separation of mothers from their children.

Two childless women, Helen Gurley Brown, editor of *Cosmopolitan*, and Gloria Steinem, cofounder and editor of *Ms*, have probably proven the most influential of all feminist leaders — thanks to their unlimited opportunities for promoting feminist ideology.

Helen Gurley Brown, who has been called "one of the major catalysts of the sexual revolution," had become editor-in-chief of *Cosmopolitan* in 1965, following the instant success of her book, *Sex and the Single Girl*, which idealized promiscuity and the singles' lifestyle. (She now boasts of a happy marriage of 30 years to David Brown, a movie producer.) Her other books include *Sex and the Office, The Outrageous Opinions of Helen Gurley Brown* and *Having It All*. But "having it all" has had very little to do with motherhood or children in any of the issues of *Cosmopolitan* throughout the past 25 years.

Omitting children from the lives of women in the pages of the magazine would seem to have been a deliberate rule, according to Mickie Moore, who interviewed the editor for the *Toronto Star*. When Moore asked her, "Why have you left out family in the way you see women?" the answer indicated that children could score very low on a list of women's interests. Brown, with her overwhelming influence as editor of one of the five largest-selling magazines in the United States and Canada, almost confessed that she, herself, disliked children. She said:

I don't want children, never wanted them . . . Most of my friends have children, and some of them get enormous pleasure from their children; some do not . . . I think with one child you can manage to have a brilliant career. With two children, I don't see how anybody does it, though some people manage . . .

I always felt that little children were awful to be around if you were 16 or 18 or 20 . . . I just wanted them to take the children away so we could get on with our lives.[2]

"I just wanted them to take the children away so we could get on with our lives" has certainly been an attitude promoted in women's magazines such as *Ms*, edited since 1972 by its cofounder, the beautiful, single, childless Gloria Steinem.

Steinem has proven as influential in the Women's Liberation Movement with her seductive speeches and through her television interviews as in her direction of feminist propaganda in *Ms*. In a major address delivered to 800 Canadians attending the first annual Barbara Betcherman memorial fund lecture at Toronto's Osgoode Hall Law School, she told the enthusiastic feminists that it was absolutely imperative that, to achieve their ultimate revolutionary goals, they "increase" their "subversive" actions.[3]

In Canada there are hundreds of examples of feminists employing her suggested "subversive," underhanded tactics. One blatant example came to light in January 1990, when the Ontario College of Art announced that all its 50 available teaching jobs would go to women, and that every position coming vacant in the next 10 years would also be filled by women only. An investigation showed that a small group of feminists had secured $53,000 from the Ontario government for an affirmative action task force to produce questionable figures of former hiring practices (few women had been applying) and then managed to call a meeting at 6:45 on Halloween, when most of the teachers were trick-or-treating with their children, leaving only 39 of the 330 teachers to vote.[4]

Feminists on both sides of the border have been involved in similar "subversive" tactics, manipulating politicians and governments into introducing the bills that would legislate our three- and four-year-old children into elementary school, long before they are ready for such regimentation (according to virtually all leading pediatric psychologists).

Lesbian feminists, it seems, have always accounted for a major proportion of the feminist leadership in the National Organization of Women (NOW) in the United States and the National Action Committee on the Status of Women (NAC) in Canada, where they have certainly wielded a tremendous influence in driving apart not only men and women, but also mothers and children.

Kate Millett would bring lesbianism to the fore as a dynamic force in the Women's Liberation Movement when she became president of NOW, and the NAC executive would bring it to the fore in Canada with government funding for lesbian workshops and numerous efforts to have all homosexual couplings granted traditional-family, government-funded benefits.

Millett's *Sexual Politics,* published in 1970, became a
feminist manual as well as a national bestseller, and is
probably the most influential textbook in women's studies
courses. Yet it is inconceivable that any thinking American
or Canadian could accept her theories.

Fathers and children would be given short shrift — a father designated as a "slaver," a "legal keeper," a "sole own-
er of wife and children." The "collective professionalization
(and consequent improvement) of the care of the young,"
the author advised, would be successful in undermining
"family structure . . . contributing to the freedom of wom-
en."[5]

Nicholas Davidson in his book *The Failure of Feminism*
quotes "dozens of passages in which Millett misrepresents
technical evidence." For instance: "Wives have never been
their husbands' chattels under Anglo-American law . . .
neither legal scholars nor medievalists, who have studied
feudalism, nor anthropologists or sociologists, who have
studied marriage, could be found to support this baseless
declaration."[6]

How could society have paid attention to this lesbian
feminist with her obvious motive of destroying our traditionally happy family lifestyles by both denigrating the
male presence and daring to reroute the lives of our children, for whom she would show not the slightest understanding or concern?

That feminism is firmly rooted in socialist principles has
been proven over and over in major international studies.
In Canada, federal and provincial politicians appear incredibly intimidated by radical feminist leaders in NAC, the
dominating government lobby group.

The World Marxist Review has praised Canadian feminist
leaders for their achievements in realizing numerous socialist goals. Meanwhile, a government grant of $50,000 to
NAC in 1987 (one of hundreds), for the "development of a
position paper on equality rights," is believed to have been

used to produce 30,000 copies of a federal election kit aimed at bringing down that very Conservative government. *Feminism in Canada,* an anthology of essays and lectures, is compulsory reading in the women's studies courses across Canada. In its pages, the feminist philosophy of women such as Helen Gurley Brown, Gloria Steinem, Kate Millett and Judy Rebick, is taught with academic authority. The authors of the articles, "by label," according to the introduction, are described as:

> . . . socialist, Marxist, lesbian, radical and anarchist feminists . . . The authors all presume that feminist revolution-evolution will involve a total integrative re-structuring of society and human relations . . . [They see] their emphasis on reproduction-related and fe-male-associated values as the key to feminist social change . . .[7]

A new attitude toward children and child-bearing is the key, in the opinion of Jill McCalla Vickers, professor of political science at Carleton University in Ottawa, a former president of the Canadian Association of University Teachers, and a former federal candidate of the New Democratic Party. She wrote:

> . . . some universal statements are both useful and important to the feminist project. The statement "only women bear children" is one such, provided we also recognize 1. that it doesn't mean that women *cause* babies, 2. that it doesn't mean that all women bear children, 3. that it doesn't mean women *must* bear children, and 4. that it could well be technologically transcended.[8]

There is no doubt that many feminists graduating from the women's studies courses across the continent are now manipulating our lives and striving to bring our legislatures closer and closer to Universal Day Care — a concept that, according to several surveys, is endorsed by only 10 percent of the women in Canada.

Have North American women been incredibly stupid in allowing society to be so manipulated? Betty Friedan had told us, the majority of women across the continent, that we had been stupid in the past — those of us who had chosen husbands, and children and loving homes as our priority. We had been stupid to embrace a career that we believed was truly the most magnificent, challenging and rewarding one that a woman could have.

I suppose feminist writers such as Carolyn G. Heilbrun, professor of English literature at Columbia University in New York, finally did convince some of us that we were indeed stupid and would need to be taught by the feminist experts "how to get our heads on straight." In her book *Reinventing Womanhood*, she explained:

> Women have, in effect, been trained not to *think*, even about their own situation . . . I would argue that the quality of many women's thinking — its confined scope and unambitious character, its lack of clarity and penetration — is shaped by the passivity and submissiveness to which they have been convention-
> .ally trained . . . This same unwillingness (to think) helps to account for the role of women as conservatives in this world, as defenders of the conventional . . .[9]

She would take great pains in helping us to understand that traditional motherhood had been doomed, even in early Greek culture. Citing the murder of Agamemnon by his wife, Clytemnestra, who was in turn slain by her own daughter and son, Carolyn Heilbrun wrote of the Greek tragedy:

May we not regard the overthrow of Clytemnestra by Orestes and Electra . . . as the symbolic moment when the institution of motherhood is overthrown? Motherhood is that institution in which woman has long been enslaved . . . It is not a woman who is being symbolically murdered: it is the principle of motherhood. That principle . . . must be demythologized and ritually destroyed.[10]

She believed that Thea, the singer in Willa Cather's novel *The Song of the Lark*, was that ideal feminist heroine who "fulfills the destiny of achievement" by sacrificing all such relationships "to preserve the valuable self." But Thea herself would wonder if she had paid too high a price:

Your work becomes your personal life. You are not much good until it does. It's like being woven into a big web. You can't pull away, because all your little tendrils are woven into the picture. It takes you up, and uses you, and spins you out; and that is your life. Not much else can happen to you.[11]

I think we must no longer listen to the women trying to reinvent womanhood by denying us our motherhood. As Barbara Grizzuti Harrison said in a *Harper's* article:

What is the real work of the world? If the real work of the world is that which extends into the future, that which is not ephemeral, and that which sustains life, we are talking about poetry and bread and babies.[12]

13
The Throwaways

We know that the destiny of the whole human race lies in the hands of our precious children. We must face the fact that if so many of us continue to abdicate all personal responsibility in caring for them, in nurturing their spirits and minds as well as their bodies, our progress not only is being handicapped; eventually, it may be ground to a halt. Bringing the family together again — reuniting mothers and fathers and children — must surely be seen now as our greatest priority.

"We have in large measure washed our hands of the idea of children as a common treasure,"[1] declared Karl Zinsmeister, an associate at the American Enterprise Institute for Public Policy Research in Washington, D.C. Leland Goudge of the Toronto Children's Aid Society, along with a multitude of other pediatric specialists across the continent, has warned us that we must cope with a "lost generation of children," children in dire distress and often with appalling, and seemingly unsolvable, problems.

There are all those aborted children of potential genius;

all those magnificent human beings who will never be born because modern men and women, driven further and further apart during the feminist revolution, are simply not coming together to conceive them; all those extremely deprived children of the wealthy, the middle-class and the poor, "thrown away" daily into day care (described as "daytime orphanages" by the famous Canadian forensic psychiatrist, Dr. Elliot Barker). There are the children of true poverty, hanging on to their mothers' jeans in the food bank lineups. Perhaps the majority of these mothers are in no way responsible for their miserable plight, but simply are the victims of a society that persuaded them that it is normal and acceptable to divorce and rear children without fathers. There are the children deliberately, unnaturally denied fathers in the lesbian households. And there are the children conceived and born simply for the self-fulfillment of more affluent single mothers, or perhaps to assuage adult loneliness; they also are denied fathers.

There are the millions of children across the continent who are the grieving casualties of parental divorce, an incredible number of them, according to the latest studies, permanently scarred, emotionally unfit for adult relationships. There are our teenagers, who, freed of all moral restraints, are destroying their lives. (One little teenage mother, putting her year-old baby up for adoption, wept, "I hit my baby — I tried to be a good mother, but I'm just too young." She was 15.) The numbers of teenage boys and girls in the courts steadily rose throughout the eighties; their roster of crimes included muggings, assault and battery, intimidation, and murder, often wanton murder. Teenage runaways — from impossible home situations, a significant number of them involving step-parents — are the prostitutes and drug addicts to be found living and dying on the streets of every large city in North America. It is estimated that in the United States there are between three and five million teenagers on the streets. In Canada, 10,000 teenagers are reported to be living on the streets of Toronto alone, with the police sometimes picking up prostitutes under the age of 12.[2]

The past decade has seen a steady climb in the suicide rate among teenagers, with children under 10 known to be escaping from a harsh, unnatural society in which the care of children has developed into our lowest priority.

DAY CARE

Day care, of course, has always been a top issue in the Women's Liberation Movement, with Universal Day Care under state control, as in Communist Russia and socialist Sweden, the ultimate feminist goal. While feminist propaganda has flooded all media, dwelling on the physical and psychological needs of mothers working outside the home, the physical and psychological needs of infants, toddlers and preschoolers — their *feelings* — have rarely been considered.

Suddenly, the most renowned pediatricians and pediatric psychologists and psychiatrists throughout the Western world were agreeing publicly that we have a crisis of dangerous proportions created by our very concepts of modern child care. This is particularly true, they claimed, in North America, where statistics reveal that more than 50 percent of all mothers work outside the home, where motherhood has been designated a secondary role, and where the youngest children are entrusted to the least skilled and lowest paid members of the workforce.

When the major long-term studies indicating the adverse effects of placing children in day care were published, the earliest years of a child's life became the focus of greatest concern.

In Canada, Dr. Elliot Barker, chief of the Province of Ontario's maximum-security facility for the criminally insane at Penetanguishene and also president of the Canadian Society for the Prevention of Cruelty to Children, coined the

phrase "daytime orphanages" in describing day care centers. Children in such centers, he had found, are simply
unable to form "close, stable bonds with constantly changing and rotating caretakers, and consequently fail to develop the trust, empathy and affection that are the basic qualities of character sought in personality development." Dr.
Barker warned that "within 15 years we can be faced with
a generation of psychopaths — adults who are superficial,
manipulative and unable to maintain mutually satisfactory
relationships with others."[3]

Furthermore, a seven-year study of psychopathic behavior at the Penetanguishene facility, undertaken with determined efforts to initiate cures and rehabilitation of psychopathic criminals, had proven a failure. The perpetrators of
such crimes as murder remained remorseless and void of
empathy or sympathy for their victims, Dr. Barker reported. His studies consistently traced psychopathic behavior
directly back to childhood.

The late British pediatrician and psychoanalyst, Dr. Donald Winnicott (Europe's Dr. Spock), whose series of books
published between 1966 and 1988 are considered among
the most authoritative studies of child development, corre-
lated a child's development processes directly to average
ages.[4]

Between 15 and 18 months of age, an infant has the capacity to develop empathy. This understanding and ability
to share in another's emotions and feeling may be learned,
Dr. Winnicott was convinced, only in a "secure
attachment" between a mother and child, with "adequate
holding." Dr. Winnicott stressed that "holding" is indispensable to the emotional development of a child, and absolutely essential for developing a capacity for empathy. In
the comforting warmth of a mother's arms, the baby will
sense that he is perceived as a "good and happy" person,
and will also sense that his mother is a "good and happy"
individual. Dr. Winnicott explained that the infant, and lat-

er the child, "internalizes" these images, and will draw on them continually for comforting when the mother and that warmth are not available. These images become "the reservoir" that the child and the adult will feed on throughout a lifetime of relating, with sensitivity and understanding, to the feelings of other human beings.

Another world-renowned British child psychiatrist, Dr. John Bowlby, in his books *Attachment and Loss* and *A Secure Base: Clinical Applications of Attachment*, insists that the attachment relationship that a child forges with his or her mother from infancy is the very "foundation stone of personality."

Humans are like computers, Dr. Bowlby suggests, storing images and information. A child forming a secure attachment relationship with his mother stores a positive image of himself and his world, and in adult life will respond to situations and people based on this inner security that was primarily nurtured in a mother's arms. As he had learned to trust his mother, he will be able to trust others and be capable of establishing loving, intimate relationships with his spouse and children. As he grows up, the child will develop into a cooperative individual, possessing high self-esteem.[5]

"Your Child's Self-Esteem — The Key to Life" is the title of a chapter by Dorothy Corkille Briggs in the bestselling anthology, *Experts Advise Parents*. She writes:

Building self-esteem is *not* a side issue of parenting. It is the cornerstone to nurturing that allows children to fulfill their promise to become the most they can become . . .

When a baby is born, he comes into the world with his total uniqueness . . . but he has no identity at all . . . Whether that identity becomes positive or negative depends on what happens between that baby and his caretakers, others around him, his own com-

parisons of himself with others, and the culture he
lives in . . .

The younger the child, the more the primary caretakers, parents, relatives, teachers, are seen as god-
like. They become the looking glass that reflects who
he is . . . High self-worth rests on [his] inner beliefs: I
am unconditionally lovable . . . I am competent . . . I
can handle myself and my world . . . I have something to offer . . . I count.[6]

A baby in the unhurried arms of his mother certainly
comes to believe that he is unconditionally lovable, that he
is of prime importance in her life and therefore is someone
of great value. That baby eventually concludes: "I count."

According to pediatric experts throughout the world,
many children in day care facilities, rushed out of warm
beds in warm homes and thrust into strange arms in
strange surroundings, instinctively know that they do not
"count" — that they are indeed the throwaways in a society that has refused to listen to their cries of anguish, their
whimpering, their silent torment.

Dr. Bowlby has said that "the young child's hunger for
his mother's presence is as great as his hunger for food . . .
and her absence inevitably generates a powerful sense of
loss and anger" that progresses from "protest" to "despair"
to "detachment."[7] Many pediatric psychiatrists have come
to believe that the children who scream the loudest and
continually hit out, particularly when their mothers return
home to them, are ventilating their feelings. They have a
better chance of surviving the trauma of separation than
do the quiet, acquiescent, resigned babies and toddlers,
who will store their inner frustrations to fester throughout
their lives.

In her book *A Mother's Work*, Deborah Fallows claims
that children in day care are being depersonalized. In her
extensive studies covering day care facilities throughout

Texas, Massachusetts, Washington, D.C., and Maryland, she found the average child's experience in day care to be "frighteningly empty, full of bewilderment, tedium, and unconsoled tears," with no opportunities for "musing." Children "wander about, constantly clamoring to go to Mommy's house."[8]

In a government study reprinted in *Reader's Digest*, Karl Zinsmeister asked: "Can you substitute a paid relationship for the natural parent-child bond without seriously harming children and society? It appears the answer may be no."[9]

Of course, feminist leaders in the United States and Canada, driving toward their goal of universal child care, were up in arms over the publication of numerous books and articles that authoritatively denounced day care as having extremely adverse consequences.

When Professor Jay Belsky, a developmental psychologist at Pennsylvania State University, published his findings from four studies involving 464 infants (*Early Childhood Research Quarterly*), he was attacked unmercifully and accused of a personal bias since his wife had resigned from a professional position to raise their two sons. (Dr. Belsky simply dismissed the charge as "vulgar and inappropriate.")

The studies, later reported in *Zero to Three: The Bulletin of the United States National Center for Clinical Infant Programs*, stated:

> Early infant Day Care may be associated with increased avoidance of the mother, possibly to the point of greater insecurity in the attachment relationship, and that such care may also be associated with diminished compliance and cooperation with adults, increased aggressiveness, and possibly even greater social maladjustment in the preschool and early school-age years.[10]

In addition to his own research, Dr. Belsky cited three other major studies that confirmed his conclusions: that infants between 12 and 15 months old, who had been separated from their mothers for more than 20 hours a week, whether in an established day care center, in a family day care situation, or in their own home in the care of a nanny or a babysitter, were at risk of developing future psychological and behavioral personality problems.

University of Texas researchers, in a study of third-graders, found that children who spent their early years in full-time day care have poorer grades and poorer study skills than children who were home-reared or whose mothers were employed part-time.[11]

In an article in the *Atlantic Monthly*, Dr. Eleanor Galenson, a prominent New York City pediatric psychiatrist, speaks of the children she is seeing every day, "children whose psyches are seriously damaged in part because of a dearth of maternal attention. Putting infants into full-time day care is a dangerous practice," she warns, adding, "Psychiatrists have been afraid to come out and tell the public this, but many of us certainly know it to be true."[12]

THE PHYSICAL RISKS TO CHILDREN IN DAY CARE

Pediatric specialists across North America also know it to be true that babies and toddlers in day care are 12 times as likely to acquire and spread infectious diseases as those children being raised at home. Dr. F. A. Loda, in the journal *Pediatrics*, informed parents that they could expect children in day care to be sick nine to ten times a year with respiratory infections alone. However, the secondary bacterial complications that often develop from minor infections — bronchitis, pneumonia and others — pose the greatest danger to the child.[13]

The Journal of the American Medical Association has reported statistics, compiled by researchers at the Centers for

Disease Control in Atlanta, that show 3000 cases of meningitis contracted by children in U.S. day care facilities *every
year.* Another study found that one percent of all children
in day care contract the dread disease — "more than 12
times the rate for children who were not in day care." This
article pointed out that 10 percent of children with meningitis will die and a third will suffer long-term neurological
damage.[14]

In an article in the *Wall Street Journal,* Dr. Stephen
Hadler, reporting further findings of the Centers for Disease Control, estimated that 14 percent of all infectious
hepatitis cases in the United States can be traced directly
back to day care facilities.[15] Other studies have shown that
70 percent of all clinical cases of Hepatitis A among adults
can be traced back to day care facilities. Older siblings appear to be particularly at risk in contracting such serious
diseases from toddlers in day care.

We have always known that the ordinary childhood diseases run rampant through day care facilities and that the
problems of screening an infected child are often insur-
mountable, since long before the child becomes symp-
tomatic he may be extremely contagious. It is also true that
some unscrupulous mothers will administer Tylenol to an
offspring to mask an early morning fever.

A lack of immunity to infection in babies and toddlers
denied mother-care was first made startlingly evident by
Dr. Rene Arpad Spitz, a Hungarian-American psychoanalyst, in his book *The First Year of Life,* which chronicles the
mental and physical health of babies in a hygienically and
sociologically approved foundling home. At the end of
their first year, the babies demonstrated "the most profound psychological and physical retardation." They were
either apathetic or crying inconsolably; they were unre-
sponsive and rarely smiled; and their lack of immunity to
infection was apparent through an exceedingly high mor-
tality rate.[16]

In his world-famous book *Psychosomatic Medicine and Contemporary Psychoanalysis,* Dr. Graeme Taylor of Mount Sinai Hospital in Toronto explains that "infant researchers now conceptualize the mother-infant relationship as an interactional system that organizes and regulates the infant's behavior and physiology from birth . . . with a direct bearing on the regulation of the child's heart rate, sleep-wake patterns, enzyme levels of growth hormone, thermo-regulation and vestibular balance." Dr. Taylor has been able to connect the responsiveness of the immune system in infancy directly to later infection and subsequent susceptibility to diseases such as cancer, diabetes, liver and heart diseases.

A mother's constant loving, holding, touching — this is the tactile stimulation that serves as "the external regulator" of the child's bodily processes. And the security of her presence, her soothing of emotional distress, provide the equally important and complex psychological regulatory effects. Dr. Taylor has found that by the end of the first year, the "integration of the mind and body takes place, and this psychosomatic integration has provided the child with his own regulatory system." The failure of the mother to provide the early external regulation, Dr. Taylor warns, has the potential of altering the immune system, impairing its ability to function normally.[17]

In the forefront of all such disturbing evidence of the psychological and physiological dangers to children in day care are the hundreds of cases before the courts of children abused or injured in such settings. Insurance rates for day care facilities have risen between 300 and 500 percent since 1985, and parents are constantly advised against placing their children in centers without adequate insurance; even the legendary minor falls may have extremely serious after-effects.[18]

Barbara Hattemer, founder of the International Foundation for the Preservation of the Family, which is based in

Naples, Florida, spoke as a member of the National Task Force on Families in Crisis, and warned:

> By restructuring the mother-infant relationship through widespread Day Care . . . society itself will be restructured. If Day Care produces large numbers of insecure, anxious and angry individuals, we must expect these traits reflected in the "personality" of the culture. We must guard against raising a generation of disturbed, lonely children who cannot relate well to other people, who are without internalized values and controls, and who are more susceptible to disease.[19]

Pediatric specialists have in the past been hesitant to "speak out," as Dr. Eleanor Galenson has explained, for fear of further distressing overworked, guilt-ridden mothers.

These mothers have been taught that their self-role must always supersede their mother-role; but surely it is time that our children should also be considered — if we are to guarantee the future of our world. Surely it is time that the mothers of North America rose up to defeat those feminists, so many of them childless, who drive us relentlessly toward Universal Day Care.

Dr. Burton White, former director of the Harvard Pre-School Project and deemed the leading North American authority on the first three years of a child's life, has stated bluntly: "After more than 30 years of research on how children develop well, I would not think of putting an infant or toddler of my own into any mother-substitute care program on a full-time basis, especially a center-based program."[20]

LATCHKEY CHILDREN

In 1988 North Americans finally began to calculate the adverse effects of a mother's absence from the home during the school years, particularly during the earliest years. "Latchkey Children in Crisis," was a headline across the continent.

The National Institute of Child Health and Human Development in the United States listed 2.4 million children, ages five to thirteen, as being unsupervised by adults after school. The true number, the institute estimated, could be more than three times that figure.[21] In Edmonton, Alberta, a city with a population of 600,000, a concerned committee instituted a study, which found that 40,000 children between five and fourteen had no one to take care of them after school. These children, the committee's report stated, had become "poor students, anxious, frustrated and alienated . . . some playing hookey, running away from home . . . driven toward delinquency, drug abuse, and even suicide." Jake Kuiken, a Calgary-based child development consultant, saw "heightened levels of fear in the five- to ten-year-olds turning into a resigned depression in the teenagers." Many of these children expressed their extreme terror at entering an empty house.[22]

Dr. Eli Newberger, director of Family Development Studies at Children's Hospital in Boston, has emphasized that it is "neither safe nor psychologically healthy for children under the age of 13 to be left alone routinely." The National Safety Council in the United States has shown that 80 percent of all accidents in the under-13 age range happen to children who are left alone.

"Children under 13 simply lack the capacity to think or act clearly in an emergency," Dr. Newberger has found. "Suppose you have a fire or an intruder breaking into the house — the child needs to think through several possible options and their outcomes. Do they call the police first, take shelter first or get siblings in a safe place first? Most children are unable to reason through such situations, even if they have been given detailed instructions."[23]

Researchers at the University of Southern California's medical school, in a study funded by the National Institute on Drug Abuse, surveyed 5000 eighth-grade-students in Los Angeles and San Diego in 1989. Reporting in *Pediatrics*, the researchers stated that they found "substance abuse — the use of drugs, alcohol and cigarettes— to be twice as prevalent among latchkey children as among those children cared for after school." Nor did the sex of the children, their ethnic backgrounds, their family status, family incomes, academic performance or their involvement in sports or other extracurricular activities seem to influence the statistics.[24]

The husband-and-wife team of Professor Thomas Long of the Catholic University of America and Associate Professor Lynette Long at the American University in Washington, D.C., interviewed 400 children, 12 to 15, across the United States. The Longs concluded that teenage pregnancies invariably happened in an empty house while the teen's mother was at work. (Dr. Lynette Long, a former elementary school principal who had observed an amazing number of children wearing house keys around their necks, coined the expression "latchkey children.")[25]

The recurring proposal of lengthening the structured school day has been resisted by educators across the continent as a cruel and unacceptable solution to the "latchkey" problem. A child's exhaustion level will reach a peak at some point in the day. In the younger child, that exhaustion was formerly assuaged in the early afternoon return to a traditional home and a mother's welcoming love and care.

In that situation, a cheerful mother had the mental and physical strength for nurturing, in comparison with the tired working mothers of today. Returning home, their energy spent, their interest levels and nurturing skills dissipated, these contemporary mothers consciously or unconsciously yearn for relief — for further separation from their precious children — through an early bedtime.

If the majority of babies and toddlers in substitute mother-care instinctively know that they are the throwaways in our feminist society, with no spiritual, psychological base for building self-esteem, then certainly latchkey children must be doubly aware of their unimportance. According to pediatric experts, their instinctive reactions to rejection are seen in their behavioral problems: their hostility, aggression, lack of concentration and poor performance in the classroom.

British television star Diana Rigg (Mrs. Peel of the long-running series, *The Avengers*) was quoted as saying: "Of course I've been home with my daughter. How could I leave her? How could any mother put anything ahead of the welfare of her child? My whole life changed with the arrival of Rachel." Mothers from every level of society have been echoing her sentiments.

TEENAGERS

Getting into the head and heart of a teenager today seemed to be accomplished by Lily Tomlin in her award-winning one-woman theatrical masterpiece *The Search for Signs of Intelligent Life in the Universe*, in which she portrays the lives of 12 typical members of an anxiety-ridden society. Fifteen-year-old Agnus Angst is described by her bewildered grandparents as "a pink-haired punk who's got the manners of a terrorist and wears somethin' makes the garage door flap up." Clothed in a leather body suit, Lily Tomlin is the teenager — a latchkey kid of divorced parents, whose father's new wife has changed the locks on all the doors. Her vile language cannot disguise a confused, desperately lonely adolescent, needing to be cared for, needing to be loved.[26]

The overwhelming need of the adolescent to be understood, to be cared for, to be loved *unconditionally* — to belong somewhere — has driven many of our teenagers into the gangs that have proliferated in every major city across North America. Pediatric psychiatrists, engaged in extensive long-term studies, had concluded by the late 1980s that the majority of these children were the victims of neglect, of broken families and of a noncaring society. By 1990, half of all the 18-year-olds on the continent had indeed come from broken homes.

In the gangs, teenagers would seek "emotional nurturing," the sense of belonging somewhere — "to a sort of family" for which they had been starving. Gang members would become their "soul mates," they explained to researchers, and the recruits would soon learn to identify with the philosophy of their new role models, no matter how aberrant and antisocial. Violence in the majority of male and female gangs would be accepted as a way of life. A violent element, large or small, is known to lurk within an adolescent's psyche; it would then be allowed to surface and thrive, often fed by the glorified images on television and video. Drugs and alcohol would oil the wheels. An initiation rite in which a prospective member must endure the brutal kicking of all gang members for 30 minutes is known to be widespread.

Researchers found teenagers from all strata of society to be represented in the gangs — kids from the richest and the poorest families, from the most affluent suburbs and the most deprived neighborhoods, from white and black and native and ethnic backgrounds. There were gangs terrorizing customers in all big-city shopping malls. At the renowned Eaton Centre in Toronto, an army of security guards were unable to prevent a group of tourists from being mugged and robbed by a knife-wielding gang, although their prompt arrival did save the visitors from serious injury.[27]

A 14-year-old girl was not as fortunate when attacked by a female gang at a bus station in an affluent Toronto suburb. As her friends stood by, paralyzed by fear, the gang pummeled her, broke her nose and stole her gold chain, wallet and cassette player. The attackers were in the process of tearing the clothes off the girl's back when they were interrupted by a 19-year-old young man of exceptional courage, who was able to fight off the six "female gangsters" who punched and kicked him unmercifully, tearing his clothes to ribbons before finally fleeing. In ensuing newspaper accounts, he became known as the white knight of the Kipling bus station.

The shocking truth is that such attacks by teenage gangs became so prevalent in the 1980s that the media stopped reporting them, although the police blotters across the continent proved they were multiplying. In Toronto, a city of two and a half million people and considered relatively safe, it is estimated that there are 40 gangs of youths "swarming" through downtown streets and suburban plazas. Clothing stores are regularly invaded by menacing, often knife-wielding gangs who simply help themselves to everything they can carry, while helpless owners and clerks stand by in fear of their lives.

Compounding the problem in Canada is the Young Offender's Act, under which teenagers may not be incarcerated for more than three years. One 13-year-old gang member scoffed: "I can shoot someone and get three years — that's only a slap on the wrist." The general crime rate among male and female teenagers — including murder, armed robberies, rape, muggings (often of defenseless senior citizens) — climbed beyond 100 percent in Toronto between 1975 and 1990. In one year, 1985, 550 criminal charges were brought against young offenders under the age of 12.

In the United States, Walter B. Miller of the Harvard Law School Center for Criminal Justice, in a report financed by the Law Enforcement Assistance Administration, stated that there were at least "2,700 gangs with 81,500 members who average 12-21 years of age, who are located in the six worst cities, New York, Los Angeles, Philadelphia, Chicago, Detroit and San Francisco." These gangs have specialized in "terrorizing the public schools."

A Los Angeles official was quoted as saying that "gangs have completely taken over individual classrooms . . . Once the number of gang members in a class reaches a certain level, the teacher is powerless to enforce discipline. Students are shaken down and forced to pay for passing through a doorway, for using gym facilities, for protection from being assaulted, or even for the right to go to school." Philadelphia school authorities closed several high school cafeterias because gangs took control over access and eating.

"Out of Control Kids Put Schools in Crisis" was the top-of-the-front-page headline in a Canadian newspaper, March 10, 1990, that focused on the alarming increase in teachers leaving the profession. One extremely worried high school principal was quoted as saying:

> The situation is becoming critical. We're frightened there'll be no one to teach these kids, because nobody wants to put up with being kicked, hit, spat at, tires slashed, robbed, threatened. Or if anyone does want the job, we're afraid they'll get torn to bits because they won't know what to do.
>
> What's amazing is, the public has not connected what's going on at home with school performance. Problems at home come as attached to school children as their lunch bags . . . Children with emotional wounds don't cry. They act out instead.[28]

The heading of the feature article in a June 1989 issue of *Time* read: "Our Violent Kids: A Rise in Brutal Crimes by the Young Shakes the Soul of Society."

What *has* happened to our soul in the decades of the feminist revolution? In the separation of men and women?

In the separation of love and sex? In the separation of mothers from their precious children?

Dr. E. Kent Hayes, in his book *Why Good Parents Have Bad Kids*, states flatly: "Parental neglect is the primary force promoting the evolution of today's disturbed child." After 25 years of working with troubled, neglected and delinquent kids in prisons, reformatories and mental institutions, Dr. Hayes writes:

> There is one personality trait common to most kids who get in trouble: a very poor self-image . . . the malady is too common to ignore . . . psychiatrists and psychologists . . . say that children are not bonding with their parents. The truth is that kids can't bond with a moving target . . . It is difficult to grow up when parents are too preoccupied to parent . . .
>
> The grouchy, stressed and overworked parent is creating a deadly atmosphere at home for the children, who start to feel bad and guilty and end up with low self-esteem.[29]

Dr. Hayes told Janet Enright in an interview she reported in the *Toronto Star* that "in the past ten years there has been a 500 percent increase in the number of middle and upper class children in North America who have been admitted to a mental institution or a prison." Psychiatrists have heard distraught parents begging to have their children committed to mental institutions, and it is estimated that hundreds of children are now unjustifiably incarcerated simply on the evidence of these distraught parents, who are no longer able to cope, particularly with the drug problems.

Dr. Freda Martin, psychiatrist at the C. M. Hinks Ontario Treatment Centres, claims that "one child in six has serious emotional problems, manifested by anti-social, defiant, aggressive, frustrated behavior, resulting in a lack of concentration and poor marks in school." She has found that two-thirds of these children come from separated or blended families. Alex Thomson, president of the Ontario Association of Children's Mental Health Centres, has reported that there are 10,000 children on waiting lists for mental health services at the 85 Ontario centers that already treat 50,000 children and their families annually.[30]

A major study undertaken by researchers at the University of California Los Angeles (UCLA), published in 1987 in the *Journal of Personality and Social Psychology*, blamed "inadequate family structure" for depression and anxiety leading to drug addiction and the continuing high suicide rates among teenagers. Another UCLA study, reported in 1988 in the *Journal of Marriage and the Family*, found that a father's involvement was more important than a mother's influence in deterring children from drug abuse. In this study, "among the homes with strict fathers, only 18 percent of children used alcohol or drugs . . . among mother-dominated homes, 35 percent used drugs frequently." The tragic truth is that in our new culture, fathers are often considered expendable, particularly in divorce.

FATHERS ARE NOT EXPENDABLE

There are 15 million children in the United States without fathers. This is the country's "greatest social catastrophe," according to Nicholas Davidson, writing in the winter 1990 issue of *Policy Review*. He reports authoritative studies in which children are shown to suffer lifetime negative effects from the deprivation of the father figure.

One major study of 18,000 students in 14 states, commissioned by the National Association of Elementary School Principals, showed "lower achievement of one-parent" than two-parent schoolchildren. A joint study by researchers from Bowling Green State University in Ohio and Columbia University in New York compared the American College Entrance Examination scores of students from father-absent homes with those of students from father-present homes "and found that father-absence has a dramatic negative effect on scores, scores that could not be attributed to socioeconomic status."

Psychiatrist Alfred A. Messer, noting the higher rate of mental illness among fatherless boys, studied their "father-hunger," which was manifested in "sleep disturbances, such as trouble falling asleep, nightmares, and night terrors." Dr. Messer has also concluded that "the period between 18 and 36 months is when a boy learns to establish his physical and gender role identity," and, if deprived of the father's presence, "the result can be deeply traumatic."

Television star Carroll O'Connor, who consistently delivers subtle sermons in his hit television series *In the Heat of the Night*, told us, in a program about a young man who lost his father, that fathers certainly are not expendable. Although the young man had a caring mother, a good job and the promise of a good future, he had missed the loving curb on an adolescent's high spirits, with the result that he fell into evil companionship and was eventually involved in robberies and murder.

The other message the actor delivered in that episode was in the anguish and remorse of the young man's cousin, Virgil, the assistant chief of police in the case. The agonizing mother told Virgil that he could have made all the difference in that young man's life if he had only "cared, telephoned him, come by," replacing the father even to a minor degree.

It was a subtle plea for all male relatives and for Big Brothers to "make all the difference" in a fatherless boy's life.

THE EFFECTS OF DIVORCE

The appalling toll that divorce has taken on the lives of children in the decades of the feminist revolution has now been documented. Dr. Judith Wallerstein, founder of the

Center for the Family in Transition, based in Corte Madera, California, carried out a 10-year study of the effects of divorce on 60 families and 131 children, aged 2 to 18. Dr. Wallerstein found that divorce places "a prolonged mental, physical and emotional burden on children." In *Second Chances*, the widely respected book that grew out of her study, Dr. Wallerstein writes:

> In most crisis situations, such as an earthquake, flood, or fire, parents instinctively reach out and grab hold of their children, bringing them to safety first. In the crisis of divorce, however, mothers and fathers put children on hold, attending to adult problems first . . . with a diminished capacity to parent in almost all dimensions —— discipline, playtime, physical care and emotional support . . .
>
> The psychological needs of children do not change . . . Our fragile family structures have gotten out of sync with our emotional needs . . . The family is supposed to be an oasis, a restorative place where children and adults find respite from the stresses of the workplace and school. Home is where a preschooler hides his head in Mommy's lap. Home is where an adolescent regroups after taking risks that lead to both failures and successes. Home is an adult metaphor for a safe place.[31]

She points out that home is no longer a safe or comforting place for a child in divorce, who is as "lonely and baffled" as Elliot, the little boy in the movie *E.T.*, who makes friends with the alien creature from outer space who is also "rootless, unconnected, and lost."

Terrible anger, occasional violence and frequent continuing vengeance can easily spill over into a child's life during divorce proceedings, causing wounds that may never heal. I believe that such behavioral patterns are learned at this time, later accounting for the number of dangerously aggressive children within our school systems.

Divorce, we know, is the only answer to impossible marital conflict. However, while a mother may be blameless in initiating divorce (studies show that in 75 to 90 percent of all cases women do initiate divorce), the children of the divorce may always feel that their mother disregarded their welfare and interests at that time in their lives. They may see the part she played in the divorce as a final betrayal that they will never forgive, consciously or subconsciously. No longer able to trust her, these children may have learned to trust no one.

Is the absence of so many preoccupied mothers from homes, from husbands and from children — reflected in the breakdown of the traditional family structure — responsible for the worsening psychological and physical health of our children?

How can it not be?

Of course, there are those wonderful children who are surviving, without permanent scars, all the disadvantages in our transitional society: the trauma endured in those early years in day care; the denial of more than 20 hours a week of a mother's nurturing care. There are the children who stoically live through their nightmarish fears as victims of the latchkey era and will not carry a fear-prone psyche into adulthood; the children who rise above parental divorce with added strengths; and the uniquely gifted children who, apparently bereft of any parental guidance and companionship, draw on their own inner resources to become the most morally responsible and contributing members of a society so desperately in need of them.

The truth is that we need the gifts and abilities of every one of our children, and our efforts must be unflagging now in recovering our troubled children from all the pitfalls in a feminist era. I believe feminist ideology has denaturalized women and men, disconnecting mothers

from fathers, and mothers from their precious children ——
the children who became the throwaways. Furthermore,
we must not blame our children for their problems fos-
tered in a troubled society of our own making.

Bringing mothers and children together again must be
our aim in defeating an ideology that demands Universal
Day Care, having already decreed that caring for one's
own precious children is a secondary occupation, unwor-
thy of a woman's time and talents. We are, in fact, talking
about an occupation that has proven itself throughout the
ages to be the most magnificent, challenging, self-fulfilling
and rewarding career a woman could possibly aspire to
—— the central role in all civilized society.

14

The Homecoming

"Just a wee cot — the cricket's chirr — love, and the smiling face of her," wrote James Whitcomb Riley, describing the ultimate joy that men, women and children across North America are beginning to expect and experience as more and more women throughout the continent pack up their briefcases and their lunch kits and head back home.

Women who had forgotten how to smile are smiling again. It is as if that great burden of feminist ideology has at last been lifted off their shoulders. They now realize that they do have a choice after all: a choice that will allow them to become "natural," feminine women again, with hearts and minds and souls allowed to overflow with unreserved, selfless loving.

"I'm tired of thinking about me, me, me," an anchorwoman of a major urban network told Megan Marshall, who was interviewing women in Boston, Washington, Chicago, New York, Atlanta, Houston and Los Angeles for her book *The Cost of Loving: The New Fear of Intimacy.* The interviewer would find them unhappy, and often extremely lonely. "Every one of these women was struggling to quiet a growing fear that all this was not enough, that the Myth of Independence had led her astray." She also learned that the women who should have been the proudest and most satisfied with their accomplishments — the partners in law firms, the top journalists, the presidents of companies — were the most disillusioned. Analyzing the disillusionment and real distress of so many of them, she explained:

> The vision of a mother inseparable from her family · was replaced by a woman attached to no one; a dream of giving was replaced by a dream of doing; a life defined by connections to others was replaced by a life of solitary self-exploration.
>
> Inevitably, I learned, the second vision eclipsed the first, the self-motivated woman in tweeds . . . promising release from a life of selflessness in the home. A good many of the women I interviewed had lived up to that second vision, learning to wear the tweeds and carry the briefcases as if they'd been born to them.
>
> But they hadn't been, and that was the whole problem. Whether because the earlier dream could not be forgotten, or because it represented something basic to female nature, by the time I interviewed these women in their late twenties and thirties, parts of the mother image were beginning to haunt the woman in tweeds.
>
> "Some days I look in my closet full of carefully tailored suits, simple blouses and blue jeans for the weekend," admitted a 32-year-old lawyer, "and it makes me very sad. I don't think I would ever feel comfortable in frilly clothes again — But it's as if there's some part of me that I've had to hide even from myself."[1]

This sort of disorientation has been illustrated in other studies of feminist-inspired career women throughout all levels of society in North America. It seems they have come to realize that their dedication to "self," their striding toward their solitary goals, their shaking off of traditional considerations such as home and family — these acts have also removed them from their basic woman's nature, as Megan Marshall suggested.

It is no surprise that this disorientation would result in serious psychological problems. Indeed, these mixed emotions, the prime cause of the mental breakdowns affecting North American women in the late 1980s, accounted for the steadily increasing number of women seeking therapy.

While some women, of course, have been successful in reconciling the elemental conflict in their own psyches, other women, formerly feminist-driven women, have begun to realize that they have merely been skimming the surface of living. Their lonely lives are a shallow replacement for the "connectedness" — the glorious sense of belonging to the past and to the future through the concept of the traditional family lifestyle.

Nor is it a surprise that the physical health of mothers trying to have it all would suffer. A mother attempting to reach her feminist potential, proving her equality with men, *fulfilling herself,* would be draining away most of her mental and physical energies in the workplace. Any leftover energies would be stretched to the limit in looking after her children. Even with a spouse willing to share the load, the situation would be much the same — particularly if his labor in the workplace was mainly physical.

Physicians across the continent associate psychosomatic symptoms with numerous physical illnesses. Dr. Lorne Becker, Chief of Family Medicine at the Toronto General Hospital, in discussing the severity of the 1990 flu epidemic spoke of the psychic influences affecting our physical well-being. "Stress, loneliness have been found to lessen the capabilities of the immune system," he said, adding that "an emotionally healthy, well-functioning family will have less incidence of illness."[2]

Professor James Laxer, a political scientist at York University in Toronto, was quoted in a newspaper article as saying: "It's just plain murder what we're going through now. This style of family is a disaster, and we're getting short-changed at both ends — home and work."[3]

Bette Davis in her last interview, shortly before her death in 1989, regretting her failed marriages and unhappy motherhood, stated: "Serious actresses shouldn't have any children unless they're willing to give up their careers. The belief that a woman can have everything — career, husband, children — is a delusion. It can't be done."[4] Anne Murray, Canada's most famous popular singer, has repeated decisively: "Children need mothers at home — and I think the teen years are the most critical — I will only schedule concerts around the timetables and needs of my teens."[5] Many mothers of teenagers work part-time only if they are able to be home at 3:00 or 4:00 p.m. They realize that a mother's comfort and understanding may be needed most when their children return home from the triumphs or failures of the day.

Restoring the "emotionally healthy, well-functioning family" can be accomplished by bringing mothers and children together again in a stable environment. Children will feel secure in a mother's devotion and loving presence, and, through the week, neighborhoods will come alive again with laughter and the sounds of kids at play. (I have heard Penelope Leach speak sadly of suburban neighborhoods that, through the week, turn into "sterile wastelands.")

History has proven that such families were responsible in the building of our great nations; in producing world-civilizing forces during war and peace; in establishing moral strengths and motivation to sustain a healthy, viable society.

George Gilder, one of the most respected and widely read economists in North America (his articles run in the *Wall Street Journal, National Review,* and he is the author of bestselling books including *Wealth and Poverty* and *Men and Marriage*), has blamed much of our frightening social conditions — the alienation of the sexes, the violence, the poverty — on the feminist revolution that has so obviously brought about the breakdown of the nuclear family.

He has argued that the very economic stability of North American society is dependent on "intact" families, and that "a civilized and productive society depends on the nurturing of children by a mother in the home and a father as provider." He explains:

> There is no way to shunt off child care to society . . . Public facilities, no matter how costly, can never substitute for the commitment and the care that mothers voluntarily provide . . . Raising children to be productive and responsible citizens takes persistent and unrelenting effort . . .
>
> The statistics show that married men are the driving force of economic growth . . . commit themselves to the future . . . work 60 percent more than single men do . . . work far harder and exploit their earnings capacity much more fully than married women or single women or single men.
>
> At the same time, it takes the kind of commitment which women routinely and readily make to their children to sustain both the man's effort and to create a new generation of men and women capable again of sustaining a prosperous and civilized society.[6]

Of course, we must consider all the single mothers, so many of them urgently in need of our sympathies and unflagging support systems. According to census figures, single mothers head 25 percent of all households on the continent. Many of them, desperately disadvantaged, are now seen simply as victims of the feminist revolution that successfully established "the single cult."

Our extreme concerns, however, for the sufferers — for the men, women and children who became the true victims of feminist ideology — must not deter us from putting the concerns of our future generations *first*. How else can we secure the future of our civilization?

Giving mothers and fathers and children back their traditional roles — with new understanding, with a new idealized vision — we may be able to restore the family to its former glory. Having come through the fires and no longer satisfied with a pinchbeck existence, we are ready to rebuild it to its former stature, with the moral strengths that made the family the very bulwark of our nation as well as the source of all our comforts and joys.

ADDENDUM

Marie, a 36-year-old cousin living in a small city in Ontario, could not be denied when she asked: "May I contribute to the 'Homecoming' chapter? I believe I am the typical homecomer." She wrote:

> I have been a full-time homemother now for over two years, and this past year, with the baby, has probably been the happiest year of my life. But when I quit my job — a really great job, a department manager with a fat salary — I was really a lost soul, set adrift, not at all sure I was doing the right thing.
>
> To begin, I was terribly lonely. I missed the hustle and bustle of that big prestigious firm, as well as some really close pals with whom I usually had

lunch; I shouldn't mention anything trivial, but I did
miss my super clothes. I was lethargic, because I
didn't have to leap out of bed every morning, waking
and dressing and dragging the kids downstairs by
6:30, while Doug made breakfast. I simply vegetated
in a housecoat for a couple of hours. Worst of all, I
was hovering over Mikey — actually plaguing him, I
can see now, with new games, outings, music class,
swimming class at the Y — never letting him out of
my sight.

While Mikey's mental health may have depended
on me to be nearby, I came to realize that even a
three-year-old needs his own space and could be
blissfully happy just muddling with his toys. Toddlers
all fantasize — the little truck drivers make deals with
the fire chief . . . I guess we went overboard on the
toys.

Of course, it was a troubled Mikey that had trig-
gered our earth-shaking decision that was to make
me a homemother. There were four horrendous
months when Mikey would wail as we left him at and
picked him up from day care, would have at least
one major crying bout before we got him off to bed
and another one during the night. It was the sound of
the crying that made us frantic with worry. It was no
normal two-year-old tantrum, but more like the wail
of a wounded animal, and I actually took to giving
him Tempra from time to time, so that the rest of us
could get some sleep.

Then we began reading those newspaper reports
about all the children with serious emotional problems, and we began to suspect that Mikey's wailing
was no passing phase. The pediatric psychiatrist we
took Mikey to was thorough and explicit. He told us
that Mikey was simply reacting to mother-loss. He believed the feminists were ready to boot him out of

town, but he had started to tell a lot of mothers to consider "going home," if at all possible; that overly sensitive babies and toddlers, especially, were at risk in day care. (We had been paying $15,000 a year for what we considered "superior" day care. My mother had looked after Emma and had taken up all the slack, but Dad recently retired, and they're now off on extended holidays.) The psychiatrist also told us that little boy preschoolers are definitely more "emotionally vulnerable" than the little girls.

The truth is, Doug and I had never thought much about the feminist bit. We had simply gone along with every other couple we knew at that time, living an average couple's average life in the 1980s. Like other mad hatters, we raced the kids out of the house in the mornings and back in at night, trying for some kind of "connectedness" in the two or three hours left in their day. Even before Mikey's problems, I suspect, we had begun to wonder if this superwoman, superman stuff had been dreamed up by idiots.

I remember I was constantly yelling at Doug for not doing enough. All of us must have unconsciously got that message: "Crack the whip until 'equality' reigns in the home as well as in the workplace." If Doug ever came home claiming overwork and exhaustion, I could top him every time.

When I look back, the guy always did his part, even cancelling a lot of cases that involved weekend commitment; he was lucky to be in a small firm that would allow it. Our sex life was a disaster — what could you expect? I was always deadbeat, if he wasn't, and I'll bet we weren't catching a spark more than three times a year. There can only be one reason a lot more husbands don't turn on their heels with a "So long, Babe": they adore their children as much as, if not more than, we mothers do.

Can anyone imagine the change in Doug's life when I came home to take over all the family and home responsibilities? Within these two years, he has been made a partner in his law firm, taking on those extra time-consuming commitments. He's a natural gardener — after all, he was brought up on a farm — and we ate vegetables out of the garden last year from July to October. And now he's making us a really great recreation room in the basement. There is no doubt that Mikey is blossoming, with his little hammer banging away alongside his dad's.

I'm not going to say that learning to be a homemaker was not a tremendous challenge, and I won't deny that it was the biggest thing I had ever tackled in my life. Furthermore, I can't help wondering if those women who still ask "aren't you bored stiff?" and "when can you get back to work?" have the faintest idea of what a homemother's job is all about. I guess I didn't, either.

You create it. That's the big difference between the homemother's job and the usual job outside. And it takes all the talents and skills you can muster. In fact, anyone who imagines that you leave any of your talents or skills or education or training out on the doorstep behind you, is simply a fool.

You keep on learning. I carry Penelope Leach around in my pocket, but also you begin to "develop your instincts" (my mother's advice). I knew instinctively that we had a problem with Emma this year, but, thank heaven, I had the time to talk a lot with her teacher and the principal at school. Emma had been put into an advanced class and was miserable until we moved her back into the mainstream, where she's now the happiest little kid in the class. I've also become very involved with the PTA, and love knowing exactly what is going on in our school.

I simply can't tell you how many ways our lives have — expanded. For instance, I used to play the piano. With my last paycheck, I bought a really good piano, and now I love helping Emma with her practicing. Doug talks about starting a midget soccer team in the neighborhood, when Mikey's about six. We've always wanted a dog, and now we have Poppy, and what unadulterated joy he has brought into all our lives. Doug and I take turns teaching Sunday school.

Of course, we could always use more money; who couldn't? My salary was bigger than Doug's, and he still doesn't make what I made. Being in a small firm, where he likes to be, there aren't the big cases that pull in the fees. But we save a lot on the day care, and my clothes, and the money we used to spend on my car, and our meals out.

We had always stayed pretty close to my family, but Doug's mother and father now treat me as if we had given them more than ten million dollars — and we have. There's a lot of visiting back and forth, and Emma calls both grandmas every day. We have friends over to dinner when we're not too tired after those night feedings with the baby, and I'm getting to be a really decent cook. And do you know, when I whip up something that Doug and the kids go wild over, I'm sometimes as happy as that woman climbing up Everest.

I've found four great friends right here in our neighborhood — three homemothers all with little kids, and one part-timer, and we have morning coffee once in a while. "Morons with their little kaffee-klatsches." I remember I hadn't paid any attention when I heard a downtowner make this remark back when I might have believed it. What we do in those kaffee-klatsches is to sort out all the weird little-kid problems that are usually too trivial to take to our pediatrician. I didn't even know that Mikey had impetigo until Alice spotted it spreading down his chin. Can anyone understand the relief I feel now when one of the kids roars up a temperature, and I know Doug and I won't have to battle about who stays home and who goes to work in an agony of worry?

I don't think I can describe exactly what has happened to Doug and me — we've grown so close, it's a bit eerie — especially after the baby. And how Emma and Mikey love their baby. In fact, our family has drawn together in a perfect little circle — our own perfect little circle — *our family circle* — so safe, so precious to each of us, I'm sure we will be holding fast to it all our lives.

This is what homecoming is all about.

EPILOGUE

Donahue on January 11, 1990, centered on an Ann Landers survey in which 70 percent of the parents responding had written: "If we had it to do over again, we would not have children." As panel and callers commented on the appalling problems in raising children in modern feminist times, Phil Donahue himself asked: "Do we have a lost generation of children?"

Do we have a lost world — a society that is so far out of sync that we are trembling even for our immediate future?

Helene Deutsch, the internationally famous Freudian psychoanalyst, was confronted in a 1972 interview by feminists questioning her early writings on female psychology. The 87-year-old Dr. Deutsch exclaimed: " — not wanting children? Oh, how sad! Oh, God, how sad . . . something is not quite right if a woman doesn't want a man or a baby . . ."[1]

We know from the history of the world that "a woman has always wanted a man and a baby"; that is, until radical feminists, many of them lesbian, took command in the

feminist revolution. That revolution has surely been responsible for the denial of morality — in the licentious-
ness, the wild promiscuity, the sexual liberation that was
always a factor in the decline of other great civilizations,
such as that of the Roman Empire. This feminist revolution
would project the demise of the traditional North American
family, in driving women from their husbands and their
homes and, most cruelly, in separating mothers from their
precious children.

The truth is, the majority of men and women throughout North America no longer seem willing to accept such
feminist ideology — to be ruled by feminist principles that
have denaturalized and disoriented men and women and
children during the past decades. Studies undertaken by
academic experts across the continent are proving conclu-
sively that we are no longer willing to accept the terrible
hurting that comes with the alienation of the sexes and the
fearful physical threats that come with the promiscuous
lifestyles and the breakdown of morality. Nor are we willing to accept the wrenching distress of so many of our lost
children.

The yearning of women for romance is seen in the millions of romance novels sold weekly to women: 202 million a year by Harlequin Books alone. The yearning of
men and women for "connectedness" and community is
translated in the searching for mates in the singles clubs of
every community on the continent. Chastity, no longer a
word to be scoffed at, is part of a restored practice in a
trustful relationship. Motherhood is back in style: motherhood on all fronts.

Stepmothers and stepfathers who make up a significant
proportion of the population are seen now to be playing a
particularly important role in turning the tide, in bringing
back stability into the lives of troubled children and society
as a whole. We remember that when Abraham Lincoln
said, "All that I am or hope to be, I owe to my angel moth

er," he was speaking of his adored stepmother, Sally, a wonderfully affectionate and cheerful widow who married his widower father when the boy was nine years old. Sally was to love him and his sister as much as she loved her own three children; sensing great potential in her stepson, she provided him with the encouragement, support and inspiration that, he claimed, would lead him to the presidency.[2]

Did anyone ever doubt that the hand that rocks the cradle rules the world?

As we are returning to fundamental truths, it would seem that the Wellesley College women who refused to invite Barbara Bush to their 1990 graduation ceremonies because she symbolized simply a wife and mother in the White House, had become intellectually hidebound, out of step. The invitation was extended only when Raisa Gorbachev was included, but did the students not realize that both women represented the "team" — that they were winning team players in the world arena?

In a memorable speech, the First Lady urged those Wellesley graduates to search beyond themselves for the true values, for the honor and joys in cherishing others. "At the end of your life," she said, "you will never regret not having passed one more test, or not winning one more verdict, or not closing one more deal. What you will regret is the time not spent with a husband, a child, a friend or a parent."

We are all being challenged in making the 1990s the Decade of the Family. Bringing men and women together again, bringing love and sex together again, bringing mothers and children together again in *the family* — the very fountainhead of all joys and strengths since the beginning of time — will give us back our future.

REFERENCES
AND
FURTHER READING

INTRODUCTION

1. George Gallup III, Empire Club Speech, Toronto, March 7, 1985.

2. Betty Friedan, *It Changed My Life* (Random House, New York, 1976), pp. xiii, xiv, xix; seminar, University of Florida, February 1985.

3. Michel Foucault, *History of Sexuality*, three volumes (Pantheon, New York, 1978, 1986).

4. Nicholas Davidson, "Life Without Father: America's Greatest Social Catastrophe," in *Policy Review* (New York, 1989), quoting from a study by The American Academy of Child and Adolescent Psychiatry, and from the *American Journal of Sociology* and *Psychology Today*.

5. *Toronto Star,* June 21, 1985.

6. CTV, November 19, 1990.

7.   Lena Beryl Associates.

8.   *Orlando Sentinel*, September 4, 1988.

9.   Nicholas Davidson, "Life Without Father: America's Greatest Social Catastrophe."

10. *Time*, January 5, 1987, p. 16.

11. *Newsweek*, November 19, 1990, p. 9.

12. Ibid.

Further Reading

Sylvia Hewlett, *A Lesser Life: The Myth of Women's Liberation in America* (William Morrow, New York, 1986).

Lynne Segal, *What Is to Be Done About the Family* (Penguin, London, in association with the Socialist Society, 1983).

Judith S. Wallerstein, Sandra Blakeslee, *Second Chances: Men, Women and Children a Decade After Divorce: Who Wins, Who Loses — And Why* (Ticknor and Fields, New York, 1989). Considered the most comprehensive study of all family members after divorce, this book documents particularly the disorientation and the lasting wounds of the children.

1   COMING TOGETHER TO TALK: DISILLUSIONED WOMEN, NEUTERED MEN

1.   Friedrich Engels, *The Origin of the Family, Private Property and the State* (International Publishers, New York, 1942).

2.   *Toronto Star*, May 11, 1990.

3. Kate Millett, *Sexual Politics* (Ballantine Books, New York, 1970), pp. 35, 86, 87.

4. Nicholas Davidson, *The Failure of Feminism* (Prometheus Books, Buffalo, N.Y., 1988), pp. 53, 64, 67.

5. Lionel Tiger, *Men in Groups* (Random House, New York, 1969).

6. Ruth R. Wisse, "Living with Women's Lib," *Commentary*, August 1988.

7. Nicholas Davidson, "Behind the Lace Curtain," *Policy Address*, 1990. Amy Clark, "80s Lingo," *Orlando Sentinel*, January 6, 1989. *Newsweek*, "Thought Police — Watch What You Say," December 24, 1990.

8. Mildred Istona, "Women MPs: Edging Steadily Toward Parity," *Chatelaine*, April 1989.

9. *Sisterhood Is Powerful*, Ed. Robin Morgan (Random House, New York, 1970), pp. 514-516.

10. *Sarasota Herald Tribune*, February 1, 1986.

11. Nicholas Davidson, "Behind the Lace Curtain," pp. 2, 3.

12. Ibid.

13. Ibid.

14. Manis Friedman, *Doesn't Anyone Blush Anymore?* (Harper and Row, San Francisco, 1990).

15. Nicholas Davidson, "Behind the Lace Curtain."

16. Ibid.

17.   Ibid.

18.   *New Dimensions*, July 1990, p. 33.

19.   Ibid.

20.   Michael McAteer, religion column, *Toronto Star*, January 20, 1990.

21.   *New Dimensions*, July 1990, p. 24.

22.   Sharon Drache, *Ritual Slaughter* (Quarry Press, Ottawa, 1989).

23.   *Toronto Star*, March 24, 1990.

24.   R. D. Kernohan, "The Churches' Real Crisis," *For a Change*, January 1991.

25.   Douglas Small, *Global TV*, April 2, 1989.

26.   *Globe and Mail*, June 27, 1987.

27.   Warren Farrell, *The Liberated Man* (Random House, New York, 1974).

28.   Warren Farrell, *Why Men Are the Way They Are* (McGraw-Hill, New York, 1986).

29.   *Globe and Mail*, February 25, 1989.

30.   *Men in Feminism,* Eds. Alice Jardine and Paul Smith (Methuen, New York, 1987).

31.   Ibid.

32.   *New Dimensions,* July 1990; from *USA Today,* p. 27.

Further Reading

August Bebel, *Woman Under Socialism*, trans. Daniel De Leon (Schocken Books, New York, 1971).

Allan Bloom, *The Closing of the American Mind* (Simon and Schuster, New York, 1987).

Madeleine Gagnon, "My Body in Writing" (translation by Wendy Johnston), in *Feminism in Canada* (anthology), Eds. Angela R. Miles, Geraldine Finn (Black Rose Books, Montreal, 1982), reprinted from *La venue a l'écriture* (Editions 10/18, Paris). Attempts "to discover/create out of our historical silence and experience, a specifically female voice" (pp. 19, 269).

Carol Gilligan, *In a Different Voice: Psychological Theory and Women's Development* (Harvard University Press, Cambridge, 1982).

Michael Levin, "Feminism and Thought Control," *Commentary*, June 1982. "The Impact of Feminism on Primary Education," in *Gender Sanity* (anthology), Ed. Nicholas Davidson (University Press of America, Lanham, Md., 1989), stated: "Feminist pedagogy covers every aspect of schooling. The efforts to change the classroom begin with the guidelines issued to authors of textbooks . . . Virtually identical in substance, wording, and format, these guidelines are in fact not suggestive but mandatory, as authors who do not follow them quickly discover . . . South-Western is as explicit as textbook publishers are likely to be when endorsing what amounts to Plato's 'Noble lie' approach to education: 'Emphasis is on what can be and should be rather than mirroring what the society is.' This double standard for accuracy permits the plea of realism to defend the portrayal of trends agreeable to feminists . . . Unsurprisingly, the very distinction between truth and falsity is quickly lost" (pp. 83, 84).

Caroline Moorehead, "A Talk with Simone de Beauvoir," *New York Times Magazine*, June 2, 1974, pp. 16-22.

Rosemary Radford Ruether, "Radical Victorians: The Quest for an Alternative Culture," in *Women and Religion in America*, Vol. 3, Eds. Rosemary Ruether and Rosemary Skinner Keller (Harper and Row, San Francisco, 1986).

Merlin Stone, *When God Was a Woman* (Harcourt Brace Jovanovich, New York, 1978).

Paul C. Vitz, *Censorship: Evidence of Bias in Our Children's Textbooks* (Servant Books, Ann Arbor, Mich., 1986).

Frank Zepezauer, "Rediscovering Masculinity: The Strange Case of Henry Higgins," in *Gender Sanity* (anthology), Ed. Nicholas Davidson (University Press of America, Lanham, Md., 1989), pp. 59-67.

2 HOODWINKING WOMEN: THE FIRST FALSE PREMISE

1. Betty Friedan, *The Feminine Mystique* (Dell Publishing, New York, 1963), p. 293.

2. Ruth R. Wisse, *Commentary,* August 1988.

3. Janet Scott Barlow, "Motherhood and the Women's Movement," *Commonweal,* September 23, 1983, pp. 489-491.

4. Dan Seligman, "The Day Care Follies," in his column "Keeping Up," *Fortune,* February 15, 1988.

5. Clara Zetkin, "My Recollections of Lenin, An Interview on the Woman Question," *Feminism,* Ed. Miriam Schneir, pp. 335-343.

6. *Toronto Star,* March 3, 7, 1989.

7. Ibid., May 11, 1990.

8. *TV Ontario,* June 1988.

9. *Financial Post,* March 14, 1988, p. 22.

10. Ibid.

Further Reading

Margaret Andersen, *Mother Was Not a Person* (Black Rose Books, Montreal, 1979).

Judith M. Bardwick, *Women in Transition: How Feminism, Sexual Liberation, and the Search for Self-fulfillment Have Altered Our Lives* (Holt Rinehart and Winston, New York, 1979).

Helene Deutsch, *Confrontation with Myself* (W. W. Norton, New York, 1973).

Deborah Fallows, *A Mother's Work* (Houghton Mifflin, Boston, 1985).

George Gilder, *Wealth and Poverty* (Basic Books, New York, 1981). Also, in "The Myth of the Role Revolution," in the anthology, *Gender Sanity,* Ed. Nicholas Davidson, he cites a Louis Harris Public Opinion Poll of 1982, in which only 12 percent of the women canvassed wanted full-time employment.

Elizabeth Janeway, *Cross Sections* (William Morrow, New York, 1982).

Juliet Mitchell, *Psychoanalysis and Feminism* (Vintage Books, New York, 1975).

Phyllis Schlafly, *The Power of the Christian Woman* (Standard Publishing Company, Cincinnati, Ohio, 1981). The author, credited with the leadership of American women in defeating the Equal Rights Amendment, discusses the continuing threat of legislation that would sound the death knell of the traditional family.

3   TOPPLING PATRIARCHY: THE SECOND FALSE PREMISE

1.   *Sarasota Herald Tribune,* March 1, 1990.

2.   *Encyclopaedia Britannica,* Vol. 23, 1962, p. 708.

3.   *Financial Post,* December 12, 19, 1988.

4.   *Toronto Star,* March 28, 1989.

5.   Ibid., January 22, 1984.

6.   *Globe and Mail,* March 17, 1986.

7.   Carolyn G. Heilbrun, *Reinventing Womanhood* (W. W. Norton, New York, 1979), p. 111.

8.   C. G. Jung, *The Undiscovered Self* (Little, Brown, Boston, 1957), pp. 71, 72.

9.   Ernest Jones, *The Life and Work of Sigmund Freud* (3 vols., Hogarth Press, London, 1953, 1955).

10.   Betty Friedan, *The Second Stage* (Summit Books, New York, 1981), p. 138.

11.   Barbara Yates, *Alumni Gazette,* University of Western Ontario, Spring 1988.

12.   Nancy G. Heller, *Women Artists: An Illustrated History* (Abbeyville Press, New York, 1987).

13.   *International Encyclopaedia of Women Composers* (Books and

Music, U.S.A., New York, London, 1988), reviewed in the *Toronto Star*, July 23, 1988.

14. Denis Donoghue, *Men in Feminism*, p. 147.

15. John Ruskin, *Sesame and Lilies: The Two Paths* (J. M. Dent and Sons, London, 1907), pp. 50, 51.

16. George Gilder, *Sexual Suicide* (Quadrangle, New York Times Book Co., 1973), quoted in *Ms*, April 8, 1983, p. 49.

17. Ruth R. Wisse, "Living with Women's Lib," *Reader's Digest*, reprinted from *Commentary*.

Further Reading

Ann Douglas, *The Feminization of American Culture* (Anchor Press, Doubleday, New York, 1988).

Wilson Bryan Key, *Subliminal Seduction: Ad Media's Manipulation of a Not So Innocent America* (Prentice-Hall, Englewood Cliffs, N. J., 1973).

4   RAMPANT, UNJUSTIFIED REVERSE DISCRIMINATION

1. Margaret Walters, "The Rights and Wrongs of Women: Mary Wollstonecraft, Harriet Marlineau, Simone de Beauvoir," in *The Rights and Wrongs of Women*, Eds. Juliet Mitchell and Ann Oakley (Penguin Books, New York, 1976), p. 352.

2. *Toronto Star*, July 3, 1987.

3. *Globe and Mail*, February 21, 1990.

4. Ibid., July 13, 1988.

5.   *Toronto Star,* December 10, 1989.

6.   *Canadian Medical Journal,* July 1988.

7.   *Toronto Star,* January 9, 1990.

8.   *Globe and Mail,* May 22, 1986.

9.   *Sarasota Herald Tribune,* November 11, 1986.

10. *Globe and Mail,* March 6, 1987.

11. *Toronto Star,* March 15, 1987.

12. *Globe and Mail,* May 14, 1983.

Further Reading

Edmund Dahlstrom, *The Changing Roles of Men and Women* (Beacon Press, Boston, 1971).

Midge Decter, "Liberating Women: Who Benefits?" in *Commentary,* March 1984. "Judges have shown themselves to be particularly susceptible to all the items on a rapidly expanding roster of fashionable social theories, and they, in turn, have succeeded in convincing many employers of the costly but convenient virtues of compliance with their findings. But husbands, teachers, colleagues, and classmates?" (p. 31).

Michael Finn, "The Earnings Gap and Economic Choices," in *Equal Pay for Unequal Work: A Conference on Comparable Worth,* Ed. Phyllis Schlafly (Eagle Forum Education and Legal Defense Fund, Washington, D.C., 1984).

Steven Goldberg, *The Inevitability of Patriarchy* (William Morrow, New York, 1973).

5 THE UGLY FACE OF ANDROGYNY

1. Mona Charen, "The Feminine Mistake," *National Review*, March 23, 1984, pp. 24-27.

2. Margaret Mead, *Sex and Temperament in Three Primitive Societies* (William Morrow, New York, 1963).

3. Derek Freeman, *Margaret Mead and Samoa* (Harvard University Press, Cambridge, Mass., 1983).

4. Margaret Mead, *Aspects of the Present* (William Morrow in conjunction with *Redbook*, New York, 1980).

5. Nicholas Davidson, *The Failure of Feminism*, p. 188.

6. *Toronto Star*, March 2, 1988.

7. *Chatelaine*, August 1987.

8. *Toronto Star*, March 8, 1987.

9. Ibid.

10. *National Geographic*, January 1979.

11. *Toronto Star*, May 13, 1988.

12. Ibid., May 26, 1989.

13. Ibid., April 28, 1988.

14. *Globe and Mail*, September 13, 1988.

15. Ibid.

16. *Toronto Star,* February 16, 1986.

17. Michael Levin, *Feminism and Freedom* (Transaction Books, New Brunswick, N.J., 1987).

18. Michael Levin, "Comparable Worth: The Feminist Road to Socialism," *Commentary,* September 1984, pp. 13-19.

19. Janet Radcliffe Richards, *The Skeptical Feminist* (Routledge and Kegan Paul, London, 1980).

20. *Newsweek,* April 22, 1985, p. 57.

21. *Maclean's,* October 1, 1984.

22. *Toronto Star,* July 13, 1989.

23. *Harvard Business Review,* February 1989.

24. *Business Week,* March 20, 1989, p. 129.

25. Anonymous.

26. CBS Television, August 24, 1989.

27. *Vital Speeches of the Day,* April 1, 1985, p. 383.

28. *Calgary Herald,* October 9, 1988.

29. *Toronto Star,* April 28, 1988.

30. Ibid., January 22, 1988.

31. Genevieve Henderson, "Women Endure Desert Life," *Colorado Springs Gazette Telegraph,* October 30, 1990.

32. *Los Angeles Times,* September 6, 1990.

33. *Toronto Sun,* March 31, 1989.

34. *Toronto Star,* November 5, 1989.

35. Ibid., January 30, 1989.

36. Ibid., August 5, 1989.

37. *Time,* February 15, 1988.

38. *Sarasota Herald Tribune,* November 9, 1989.

39. Ibid.

40. *Health Watch Report,* Ed. Gene Antonio, March-April 1989.

41. *Globe and Mail,* August 7, 1987.

42. *Toronto Star,* August 5, 1989.

43. Brian Mitchell, *The Weak Link: The Feminization of the American Military* (Regnery Gateway, Washington, D.C., 1989).

44. *Globe and Mail,* April 7, 1990.

45. *Toronto Star,* March 22, 1990.

46. *Maclean's,* April 10, 1989, p. 9.

47. *Chatelaine,* February 1990.

Further Reading

Roland Barthes, *Mythologies,* translated from the French by Annette

Lavers (Granada Publishing, London, 1981). The most widely quoted
passage: "Women, be therefore courageous, free; play at being men . . .
but never get far from them . . . always remember that man exists, and
that you are not made like him . . . first acknowledge the obligations of
your nature . . . don't forget . . . to produce children, for that is your
destiny . . ." (pp. 50-52).

Yves Christen, "Sex Differences in the Human Brain," in the anthology
Gender Sanity, is a translation of Chapter 13 in *L'égalité des sexes: L'un
n'est pas l'autre* (Editions du Rocher, Monaco, 1987). This is a
comprehensive report of the findings of leading European behavioral
scientists proving the differences — psychological, mental and physical
— between men and women, to deny androgyny.

Nicholas Davidson, "Feminism Deconstructs Itself," *National Review,*
August 20, 1990.

V. R. Fuchs, "Sex Differences in Economic Well-being," *Science,* April
1986.

Weldon M. Hardenbrook, *Missing from Action: Vanishing Manhood in
America* (Thomas Nelson, Nashville, Tenn., 1987).

Christopher Lasch, *The Culture of Narcissism: American Life in an Age of
Diminishing Expectations* (W. W. Norton, New York, 1978).

Judith Ochshorn, "The Contest Between Androgyny and Patriarchy," in
Feminist Visions, Eds. Diane L. Fowlkes and Charlotte S. McLure
(University of Alabama Press, Tuscaloosa, 1984), pp. 74-83.

Melford E. Spiro, *Gender and Culture: Kibbutz Women Revisited*
(Schocken, New York, 1980).

Arianna Stassinopoulos, *The Female Woman* (Random House, New
York, 1973).

Lionel Tiger, Joseph Shepher, *Women in the Kibbutz* (Harcourt Brace Jovanovich, New York, 1975).

6 STRIPPING AWAY FEMINISM'S FALSE FACES

1. *Toronto Star,* February 23, 1989.

2. *Saturday Night,* May 1988, p. 35.

3. *Women's Organizations and Leaders Directory,* Washington, D.C.

4. *Toronto Star,* October 30, 1989.

5. *Globe and Mail,* September 28, 1987.

6. *Toronto Star,* June 10, 1987.

7. Nicholas Davidson, "The Myths of Feminism," *National Review,* May 19, 1989, pp. 44-46.

8. *Sarasota Herald Tribune,* November 9, 1987.

9. *Globe and Mail,* September 24, 1987.

10. David Vienneau, "Supreme Court Smiled on Women, Natives," *Toronto Star,* July 14, 1990.

11. *Globe and Mail,* January 12, 1991.

12. *Toronto Star,* July 11, 1987.

13. Canadian Press, January 6, 1987.

14. Ibid.

15. *Maclean's,* October 3, 1988.

16. *Globe and Mail,* August 10, 1988.

17. Ann Landers, *Toronto Star,* January 29, 1989.

18. *Globe and Mail,* June 10, 1989.

19. Ibid., August 15, 1989.

20. Ibid., March 12, 1987.

21. *Saturday Night,* May 1988; *Globe and Mail,* April 23, 1988.

22. Nellie McClung, *The Stream Runs Fast* (T. Allen, Toronto, 1945).

23. *Child Abuse in the Classroom,* Ed. Phyllis Schlafly (Pere Marquette Press, Alton, Ill., 1984). A biographical sketch was included in the book, which is a collection of excerpts from the *Official Transcript of Proceedings* before the U.S. Department of Education that took place through March 1984 (p. 4).

24. Carol Felsenthal, *Phyllis Schlafly: The Sweetheart of the Silent Majority* (Regnery Gateway, Chicago, 1981), p. 197.

25. Phyllis Schlafly, *The Power of the Christian Woman* (Standard Publishing Company, Cincinnati, 1981), p. 151.

26. Ibid., p. 155.

27. Carol Felsenthal, *Phyllis Schlafly,* p. xiii.

28. Valerie Riches, *Sex and Social Engineering* (Family and Youth Concern, Wicken, Milton Keynes, Bucks, England, 1990).

Further Reading

C.T., "The Furious Feminist: Finding the Line Between Blame and Responsibility," *Ms,* February 1983, p. 81.

Andrea Dworkin, *Women Hating* (Putnam, New York, 1974).

R. J. Gelles, *The Violent Home: A Study of Physical Aggression Between Husbands and Wives* (Sage Publications, Beverly Hills, Calif., 1974).

George Gilder, *Men and Marriage* (Pelican, Gretna, La., 1986).

Marjorie Hansen Shavitz, Morton H. Shavitz, *Making It Together* (Houghton Mifflin, Boston, 1980).

Rita Kramer, "The Establishment of Feminism," in the anthology *Gender Sanity.* The author documents the violent activities and influence of the most extreme groups of feminists, such as the Redstockings, the Radical Feminists, and WITCH (Women's International Terrorist Conspiracy from Hell), some of them direct offshoots of NOW.

R. L. McNeely and Gloria Robinson-Simpson, "The Truth About Domestic Violence," in *Gender Sanity,* pp. 163-176.

Cynthia Smith, *Why Women Shouldn't Marry* (Lyle Stuart, Secaucus, N.J., 1988).

Betty Steele, "Hate and Vengeance in the Women's Movement," in *The Feminist Takeover: Patriarchy to Matriarchy in Two Decades* (Tercet, Toronto, 1987), pp. 14-25.

United Nations Report, *Women and Crime: A Virtually Neglected Social Issue,* September 1985.

ROCK AND ROMANCE — AND THE ROOTS

Myrna Kostash, *Long Way From Home* (James Lorimer, Toronto, 1980), pp. 107-114.

2. John Stuart Mill, *The Subjection of Women* (Oxford University Press, London, 1971).

3. Ibid.

4. Ibid.

5. Brock Chisholm, *Can People Learn to Learn* (G. Allen, New York, 1958).

6. A. C. Kinsey, et al., *Sexual Behavior in the Human Male* (W. B. Saunders, Philadelphia, 1953).

7. Alexander Solzhenitsyn, *Time,* July 24, 1989.

8. *Sarasota Herald Tribune,* February 1, 1986.

9. *The Lancet,* Summer 1988.

10. *Time,* June 22, 1987, p. 69

Further Reading

Ivan Boszormenyi-Nagy, Geraldine M. Spark, *Invisible Loyalties* (Harper and Row, New York, 1973).

Brock Chisholm, in *Prescription for Survival* (Columbia University Press, New York, 1957). In debunking the Ten Commandments, Chisholm cited "Honor thy father and thy mother" as particularly damaging for children. He wrote: "I do not believe in the imposing of any commandments on children . . . just because the parent has adopted a faith, it is not necessarily at all the best faith for a child . . . it should be for him to decide, not the parent . . . We feel we have a license to misinform children . . . to tell them weird things . . . Believing in fairies and Santa Claus as a wee child is conducive to irresponsible behavior later on."

Midge Decter, *Liberal Parents, Radical Children* (Coward, McCann, New York, 1975).

Christopher Lasch, *Haven in a Heartless World: The Besieged Family* (Basic Books, New York, 1977).

Michael R. Liebowitz, *The Chemistry of Love* (Little, Brown, Boston, 1983).

8   SEXUAL WARFARE

1. Kate Millett, *Sexual Politics* (Doubleday, New York, 1970). Nicholas Davidson in *The Failure of Feminism* gives a comprehensive analysis of Kate Millett's writings and influence, pp. 18-25.

2. Ibid.

3. Nicholas Davidson, *The Failure of Feminism*, p. 86.

4. *Sisterhood Is Powerful*, Ed. Robin Morgan (Random House, New York, 1970), p. 487.

5. Shulamith Firestone, *The Dialectic of Sex* (Bantam Books, New York, 1971), p. 69.

6. Simone de Beauvoir, *The Second Sex* (Vintage Books, New York, 1974).

7.   *Weekend Magazine,* September 30, 1978.

8.   Betty Steele, *The Feminist Takeover* (Tercet, Toronto, 1987), pp. 160, 161.

9.   *Maclean's,* February 27, April 16, 1984. Germaine Greer, *The Female Eunuch* (McGraw-Hill, New York, 1970); *Daddy We Hardly Knew You* (Farrar, Straus and Giroux, New York, 1989).

10   Carolyn G. Heilbrun, *Reinventing Womanhood,* p. 175.

11. Alvin Toffler, *Future Shock* (Bantam Books, New York, 1970).

12. *Globe and Mail,* April 25, 1987.

13. Ibid., June 23, 1987.

14. *Washington Post,* March 1, 1990.

15. *Chatelaine,* October 1989.

16. *Globe and Mail,* June 21, 1989.

17. *Toronto Star,* July 22, 1989.

Further Reading

Shere Hite, *Women and Love* (St. Martin's Press, New York, 1989). *The Hite Report: A Nationwide Study of Male Sexuality* (Dell, New York, 1981).

Mary Jane Sherfey, *The Nature and Evolution of Female Sexuality* (Vintage Books, New York, 1973).

Donald Symons, *The Evolution of Human Sexuality* (Oxford University

Press, New York, 1979).

9 THE ALLEY CAT SYNDROME

1. *Toronto Star,* June 4, 1988.

2. *The Phyllis Schlafly Report,* October 1986.

3. Shulamith Firestone, *The Dialectic of Sex.*

4. Carey French, "Sexual Swinging in the Plague Years," *Globe and Mail,* October 1, 1988.

5. Ibid.

6. Ibid.

7. Dr. Philip Blumstein, Dr. Pepper Schwartz, *American Couples* (William Morrow, New York, 1983).

8. *New Woman,* November 11, 1986.

9. Shere Hite, *A Cultural Revolution in Progress* (Knopf, New York, 1987).

10. *Time,* October 12, 1987, p. 64.

11. Dr. Philip Blumstein, Dr. Pepper Schwartz, *American Couples,* pp. 267-306.

12. Ibid.

13. *Globe and Mail,* September 21, 1989.

14. *Flare,* September 1989, p. 234.

15. *Ottawa Citizen,* November 11, 1989.

16. Lena Beryl Associates.

17. Ibid.

18. Ibid.

19. The *Toronto Women's Book,* Eds. Joe Currie, Jan Wendland (Macmillan of Canada, Toronto, 1989), p. 158.

20. Judy Markey, "Introducing a Hassle-Free Bed Partner," *Sarasota Herald Tribune,* November 19, 1988.

21. Ibid.

22. Cynthia Smith, *Why Women Shouldn't Marry* (Lyle Stuart, Secaucus, N.J., 1988).

23. *Glamour,* January 1989.

24. *Ladies' Home Journal,* February 1989.

25. *Cosmopolitan,* January 1989.

26. *Health,* May-June 1989, p. 116.

27. Shere Hite, *The Hite Report: A Nationwide Study of Female Sexuality* (Dell, New York, 1976).

28. Nicholas Davidson, *The Failure of Feminism,* pp. 78-81.

29. *Sisterhood Is Powerful,* p. 309.

30. Susan G. Cole, "Nicole Brossard," *Now,* September 21-27, 1989.

31. Christopher Jones, "Phranc Proffers Folksongs," *Now*, September 21-27, 1989.

32. Cited in *Men in Feminism*, p. 223.

33. *Globe and Mail*, September 19, 1989.

34. *Saturday Night*, April 1988.

35. Al Neuharth, "Plain Talk," *USA Today*, February 1989.

36. Sabina McLuhan, *Reality*, Spring 1987, quotation from *The National Review*.

37. Ibid.

38. *Globe and Mail*, September 20, 1989.

39 *Human Life International Reports*, July-August 1989.

40. *Toronto Star*, April 20, 1989.

41. *Health Watch Report*, July-August 1989.

42. *Time*, November 24, 1986.

43. *The American Journal of Diseases of Children*, August 1989 (a study of 506 teenagers by researchers at San Francisco Campus, University of California).

44. Lena Beryl Associates.

45. *Globe and Mail*, August 24, 1989.

46. Helen Puner, *Not While You're a Freshman* (Coward-McCann, New York, 1965). pp. 46-47.

Further Reading

Gene Antonio, *The AIDS Cover-up? The Real and Alarming Facts About Aids* (Ignatius Press, San Francisco, 1986).

Ernest Hemingway, *For Whom the Bell Tolls* (Macmillan, New York, 1977). *A Moveable Feast* (Macmillan, 1988). Helen Puner, a renowned Freudian scholar, in a footnote to her book *Not While You're a Freshman,* wrote: "It was in Hemingway's *For Whom the Bell Tolls* that the earth shook on account of a sexual experience . . . But I have sad news for you about Hemingway himself. When he was a young man, he wrote that what made you feel good was 'moral,' what made you feel bad 'immoral.' In his posthumous book, *A Moveable Feast,* he wrote, 'Nothing ever worked out for me morally.' . . . The point is that I don't think Sheer Unadulterated Eros Is Enough."

Dr. Stan J. Katz, Aimee E. Liu, *False Love* (Ticknor and Fields, New York, 1988), pp. 235-238.

Andrea Sachs, "Handing Out Scarlet Letters," *Time,* October 8, 1990. Anne Hopkins reported the story of a Norwich, Connecticut, man having his wife charged with adultery. This resurrected an old law that was found to be still on the books in at least half the states, including New York, Michigan and Massachusetts. In Norwich, the woman accused faced a $1000 fine and up to a year in jail. In Janesville, Wisconsin, a woman completed 40 hours of community service to avoid the expense of a trial and up to two years in jail and a $10,000 fine. In 1986, the U.S. Supreme Court had upheld the right of states to ban homosexual sodomy, and it was suggested that the adultery law may also be upheld. "Who wants to come out in public in favor of adultery?" asked Ronald Allen, a professor of law at Northwestern University.

Brooks R. Walker, *The New Immorality* (Doubleday, New York, 1968).

10   GOLDE, DO YOU LOVE ME?

1.   James Atlas in *Vanity Fair,* quoted in *Reader's Digest,* October 1986.

2.   Albert Camus, *The Plague,* translated from French by Stuart Gilbert (Hamish Hamilton, London, 1947).

3.   Maggie Scarfe, *Intimate Partners: Patterns in Love and Marriage* (Random House, New York, 1987), p. 79.

4.   Betty Friedan, *The Feminine Mystique.*

5.   Nicholas Davidson, *Behind the Lace Curtain,* quoting from Muriel Dimen, *Surviving Sexual Contradictions* (Macmillan, New York, 1986).

6.   T. S. Eliot, *Little Gidding: The Complete Poems and Plays* (HarBrace, New York, 1950).

7.   Sylvia Plath, *The Bell Jar* (Faber and Faber, London, 1963).

8.   Robin McGibbon, *New Kids on the Block: The Whole Story* (First Avon Books, New York, 1990).

9.   Ibid.

10.   Ibid., pp. 104, 105.

Further Reading

Midge Decter, *The New Chastity, and Other Arguments Against Women's Liberation* (Coward, McCann and Geohegan, New York, 1972).

Carol McMillan, *Women, Reason and Nature* (Princeton University Press,

New Brunswick, N.J., 1982).

Alice von Hildebrand, "Physical and Spiritual Ecology," in the anthology, *Feminism v. Mankind,* Ed. Christine M. Kelly (Family Publications, Wicken, Milton Keynes, England, 1990).

11   MOTHERHOOD

1.   *Toronto Star,* December 15, 1989; June 10, 1989.

2.   Betty Friedan, *The Feminine Mystique,* p. 231.

3.   Lena Beryl Associates.

4.   *Toronto Star,* March 13, 1989.

5.   Ibid., from Reuters, April 6, 1989.

6.   Ibid.

7.   *Saturday Review,* "Sex, Society, and the Female Dilemma: A Dialogue Between Simone de Beauvoir and Betty Friedan," June 14, 1975, quoted by Nicholas Davidson in *The Failure of Feminism,* p. 17.

8.   Betty Freidan, *The Second Stage,* p. 333.

Further Reading

Sylvia Ann Hewlett, "Running Hard Just to Keep Up," *Time,* December 3, 1990. Prominent U.S. economist Sylvia Hewlett discusses "The Cost of Neglecting Our Children." She cites the high mortgages that force many mothers, unwillingly, out of their homes, away from their children — "the total contact time between parents and children dropping 40 percent over the past 25 years." With 52 percent of American women working full-time, there are "ominous links between absentee parents and behavioral problems among children," she writes. She suggests that governments provide subsidized housing and lower mortgage rates for young families.

Caroline Moorehead, "A Talk with Simone de Beauvoir," *New York Times Magazine,* June 2, 1974, pp. 16-22.

12 CHILDLESS, LESBIAN SOCIALIST LEADERS IN THE WOMEN'S LIBERATION MOVEMENT

1. Betty Steele, *The Feminist Takeover,* pp. 165-174.

2. *Toronto Star,* February 2, 1989.

3. *The Feminist Takeover,* p. 177.

4. *Toronto Star,* January 12, 1990.

5. Nicholas Davidson, *The Failure of Feminism,* p. 18.

6. Ibid., p. 22.

7. Angela R. Miles, "Introduction," *Feminism in Canada: From Pressure to Politics,* Eds. Angela R. Miles, Geraldine Finn (Black Rose Books, Montreal, 1982), pp. 12, 13.

8. Ibid.

9. Carolyn G. Heilbrun, *Reinventing Womanhood,* pp. 87, 88.

10. Ibid., pp. 154-156.

11. Ibid., p. 80.

12. Barbara Grizzuti Harrison, "What Do Women Want?" *Harper's,* October 1981, p. 39.

Further Reading

Bryce J. Christensen, "The Retreat from Marriage," in *Who Will Rock the Cradle.* The author is the editor of *The Family in America* and the director of the Rockford Institute Center on the Family in America, a research organization studying all aspects of family life, which he sees to be in extreme jeopardy.

James Woodress, *Willa Cather: Her Life and Art* (University of Nebraska Press, Lincoln, 1970).

13 THE THROWAWAYS

1. Karl Zinsmeister, "Raising Children in a Difficult Age," in *Who Will Rock the Cradle* (an anthology of speeches from two conferences on child care), Ed. Phyllis Schlafly (Eagle Forum Education and Legal Defense Fund, Washington, D.C., 1989).

2. *Toronto Star,* February 12, 1986.

3. *Maclean's,* May 20, 1985.

4. Donald Winnicott, *Babies and Their Mothers* (Addison-Wesley, Reading, Mass., 1987).

5. John Bowlby, *A Secure Base: Clinical Application of Attachment Theory* (Routledge and Kegan Paul, London, 1988).

6. Dorothy Corkille Briggs, "Your Child's Self-Esteem: The Key to Life," in the anthology, *Experts Advise Parents,* Ed., Eileen Shiff (Delacorte Press, New York, 1988), p. 7.

7. John Bowlby, *A Secure Base.*

8. Deborah Fallows, *A Mother's Work* (Houghton Mifflin, Boston, 1985).

9. Karl Zinsmeister, "Hard Facts About Day Care," *Reader's Digest,* April 1989, condensed from *Policy Review,* Spring 1988.

10. *Atlantic Monthly,* August 1988, pp. 73, 74. *Toronto Star,* April 3, 1987.

11. Wendy Dreskin, "Day Care: A Child's View," in *Who Will Rock the Cradle,* p. 131.

12. *Atlantic Monthly,* August 1988, p. 73.

13. Robert Rector, "Myths and Facts About Families and Day Care," in *Who Will Rock the Cradle,* pp. 214, 215.

14. Ibid.

15. Ibid.

16. Rene Arpad Spitz, *The First Year of Life* (International University Press, London), 1966.

17. Barbara Hattemer, "New Light on Day Care Research," in *Who Will Rock the Cradle,* p. 78.

18. Betty Steele, *The Feminist Takeover,* p. 128.

19. Barbara Hattemer, "New Light on Day Care Research," p. 79.

20. Karl Zinsmeister, "Raising Children in a Difficult Age," p. 20.

21. *Toronto Star,* July 13, 1988.

22.   Ibid., August 12, 1985.

23.   *USA Today, Boston Globe, Toronto Star,* July 3, 1988.

24.   *Toronto Star,* September 9, 1989.

25.   Ibid.

26.   Royal Alexandra Theatre, Toronto performance.

27.   *Globe and Mail,* January 30, 1989.

28.   *Toronto Star,* March 10, 1990.

29.   Dr. E. Kent Hayes, *Why Good Parents Have Bad Kids* (Doubleday, New York, 1989).

30.   *Toronto Star,* February 28, 1989.

31.   Judith S. Wallerstein, Sandra Blakeslee, *Second Chances: Men, Women, and Children a Decade after Divorce: Who Wins, Who Loses and Why,* pp. 17-19.

Further Reading

Nicholas Davidson, *The Failure of Feminism,* pp. 281, 288, 328.

William and Wendy Dreskin, "Day Care and Children," in the anthology *Gender Sanity,* Ed. Nicholas Davidson (University Press of America, Lanham, Md., 1989).

Abigail Trafford, *Crazy Time — Surviving Divorce* (Harper and Row, New York, 1982), p. 200.

Marjorie U'ren, "The Image of Women in Textbooks," in *Women in Sexist Society,* Ed. Vivian Gornick and Betty Moran (Mentor, New York, 1971).

Donald Winnicott, *Human Nature* (Schocken Books, New York, 1988).

14 THE HOMECOMING

1. Megan Marshall, *The Cost of Loving: The New Fear of Intimacy* (G. P. Putnam's Sons, New York, 1984), pp. 29, 30.

2. CTV, January 12, 1990.

3. *Toronto Star,* March 7, 1989.

4. *Parade Magazine,* November 19, 1989, p. 14.

5. Anne Murray, CBC *Radio Noon,* 1988.

6. George Gilder, "Child Care in a Gender-Neutral Society," in *Who Will Rock the Cradle,* pp. 162, 163.

Further Reading

Sarah Bonnett Stein, *Girls and Boys: The Limits of Nonsexist Childrearing* (Scribner's, New York, 1983).

EPILOGUE

1. Carolyn G. Heilbrum, *Reinventing Womanhood,* p. 110.

2. Mercedes Lynch Maloney, Anne Maloney, *The Hand That Rocks*

the Cradle: Mothers, Sons and Leadership (Prentice-Hall, Eaglewood Cliffs, N.J., 1985).

3. Time, June 11, 1990, p. 22.

ACKNOWLEDGMENTS

The following have generously given permission to reprint material from copyrighted works: Avon Books, from *New Kids on the Block: The Whole Story,* by Robin McGibbon (1990), used by arrangement with Avon Books. Black Rose Books, from "Introduction" to *Feminism in Canada: From Pressure to Politics* (1982), by Angela Miles, Angela Miles and Geraldine Finn eds. *Chatelaine,* from "Women MPs: Edging Steadily Toward Parity," by Mildred Istona (April 1989), excerpted by permission. *Commonweal,* from "Motherhood and the Women's Movement," by Janet Scott Barlow (September 23, 1983). Dell, a division of Bantam, Doubleday, Dell Publishing Group, Inc., from "Your Child's Self Esteem," by Dorothy Corkville Briggs, M.S., in *Experts Advise Parents* (1987), Eileen Shiff ed. Eagle Forum Education and Legal Defense Fund, Washington, D.C., from "New Light on Day Care Research," by Barbara Hattemer and "Child Care in a Gender Neutral Society," by George Gilder, in *Who Will Rock the Cradle?* (1989), Phillis Schlafly ed. *The Globe and Mail,* from articles dated May 14, 1983, February 25, 1989, June 21, 1981. Houghton Mifflin Company, from *Second Chances,* by Judith Wallerstein and Sandra Blakeslee, copyright © by Judith S. Wallerstein and Sandra Blakeslee, reprinted by permission of Ticknor & Fields, a Houghton Mifflin Company. Leonard Cohen, Stranger Music, Inc., from lyrics from the song entitled